AIRPORT AIRSIDE AT BWI

BALTIMORE-WASHINGTON INTERNATIONAL THURGOOD MARSHALL AIRPORT

GEORGE W. HAMLIN

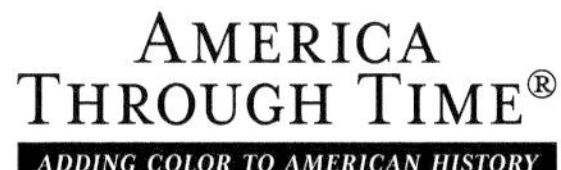
AMERICA THROUGH TIME®
ADDING COLOR TO AMERICAN HISTORY

America Through Time is an imprint of Fonthill Media LLC
www.through-time.com
office@through-time.com

Published by Arcadia Publishing by arrangement with Fonthill Media LLC
For all general information, please contact Arcadia Publishing:
Telephone: 843-853-2070
Fax: 843-853-0044
E-mail: sales@arcadiapublishing.com
For customer service and orders:
Toll-Free 1-888-313-2665

www.arcadiapublishing.com

First published 2023

ISBN 978-1-63499-489-7

Typeset in 10pt on 13pt Sabon
Printed and bound in England

Dedication

This book is dedicated to the memory of Daniel J. Breitenbach, who died in a helicopter crash on August 4, 2001, while working on a professional photography assignment. Since one of his clients was BWI airport, he was a logical choice to escort me in the AOA (Air Operations Area) during the period when most of the photos used in this book were made. Working with him was a pleasure, from both a photography perspective and on a personal basis.

Most photographers doing any sort of fieldwork know that waiting can take as much of the time, or even more, than the actual shooting. Thus, it makes a difference who you are with while doing this. An impatient escort could be very detrimental to the effort; this was never a problem with Dan, and he made it clear that he wanted me to be able to get what I needed. In addition, it was enjoyable to talk with him about a variety of subjects, including photography. I was lucky to have the chance to work with him.

Contents

Foreword

O'er the Ramparts We Watched

There was a time when airline operations were conducted out in the open, for all to see: passengers, well-wishers, and even those curious enough to go to the airport just to see what the airline business was all about. There generally was some sort of barrier—likely a low chain-link fence—between the amateurs and the working pros out with the aircraft, because the planes were, after all, dangerous machinery, particularly with respect to unwitting pedestrians. Nonetheless, there was not much that an observer could not see or, for that matter, hear or smell.

As the airline business progressed, spectators increasingly were cordoned off from the action, for reasons of both safety and congestion, at least in most locations. Beginning in the 1970s, security concerns administered the *coup de grâce*, with airside operation areas becoming controlled and restricted.

In the process, terminal concourses became "sterile" areas, with passengers more often than not afforded the luxury of boarding the aircraft via telescoping "jet bridges." The days of a rack of umbrellas at the ramp door virtually vanished, and it was not even necessary to don a coat to proceed between the comfortable environments of gate hold room and aircraft cabin.

While a distinct improvement, something was lost in the process—the intimate familiarity with the flying machines, especially for those not traveling. Sure, there were windows at most gates, but the view is often limited, and other sensory inputs have been eliminated almost entirely. At night, viewing is often difficult; in some cases, it can be virtually impossible to see the aircraft you are about to board.

Thus, today's airport user is familiar with the airport from curbside; at the ticket counter; through the security checkpoint; and, finally, the gate itself, which may actually afford a view of the *raison d'être* of the facility. The experience is limited and controlled; there is little reason to go to the airport unless you are actually traveling, or accompanying someone who is.

In a modest number of cases, especially at smaller airports, at least some of the activities can still be observed without being initiated into the world of the airline employee, made privy to the rites of the security system, and becoming the possessor of

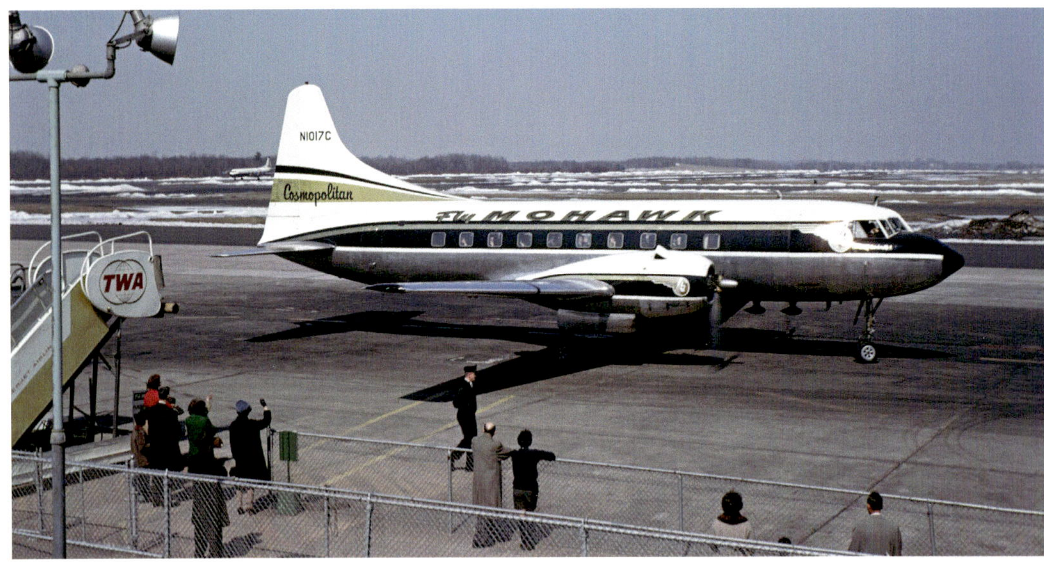

This April 1963 scene at Bradley Field, in Windsor Locks, Connecticut, which continues to serve as the airport for Hartford, Connecticut, and Springfield, Massachusetts, is typical of how airports used to be even several years into the "Jet Age." Mohawk's piston-engined Convair 240 N1017C, which the Utica, New York-based carrier had acquired from Swissair in 1957, is departing for its next destination. The people at the gate, which is both literal and outdoors, have had a full view of airport airside activities associated with N1017C's visit to BDL, the airport's three-letter code, whether they are seeing someone off, or just observing. (*Photo by Ira Ward, George Hamlin collection*)

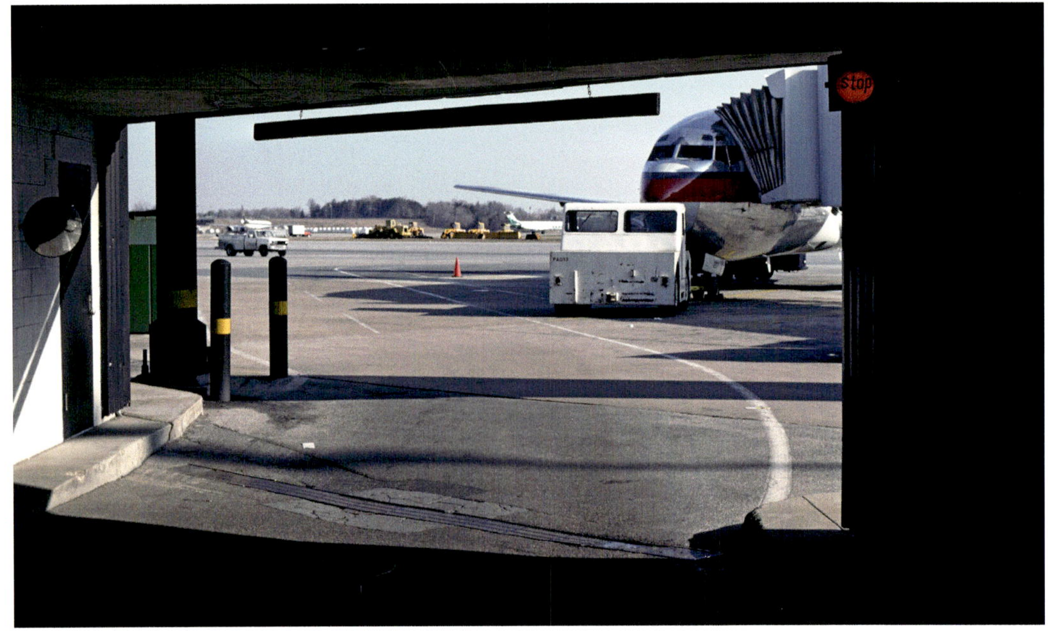

Time to go airside and step out onto the ramp to see what's going on!

a ramp badge. There are still observation decks in some locations. In others, well-placed parking garages serve a similar purpose. Recently there has been an incipient trend of opening outdoor viewing areas, which may offer some insight into what goes on airside.

Still, curiosity as to what goes on beyond the fence and security gates at airports is not satisfied for many. What is involved in the daily ebb and flow of airline operations at a major facility? How do all the activities come together to make air travel a routine, mass-travel experience? Would it not be interesting, maybe even exciting, to have an "up close and personal" view of landings and takeoffs? The ensuing sections of this book hope to provide some insight into these items, and in the process, to be able to take a look at what is still a fascinating and colorful business. Now that we are properly escorted, let us head for airside, and find out.

Introduction and Acknowledgments

In over fifty years of airline-related photography, I have had the chance to shoot at many airports, both in the U.S. and many other locations around the world. Often, I am in the same position as any other aviation enthusiast—i.e. taking photos from outside the now-secure environment where airport operations take place.

However, I have also had many opportunities in my professional career in the commercial aviation and aerospace industries to be in, and photograph from, the "AOA," or Air Operations Area, as the FAA (Federal Aviation Agency) defines it.

During the mid-1990s, it occurred to me that there might be interest in a pictorial book that showed what went on at a typical large commercial airport. I contacted a friend at BWI, who was interested in assisting me with this project.

Incidentally, since the airport is now (since 2005) known as the "Baltimore-Washington (or BWI) International Thurgood Marshall Airport," I have used that in this book's title, since most people reading it will be familiar with that description. When the photographs were being taken, it was the "Baltimore-Washington Airport," or, more often than not, simply "BWI."

While the photos were taken between 1994 and 1999, mostly towards the end of that time period, publication was postponed for a variety of reasons. As a result, while serving the original purpose I set out to achieve, it also illustrates many things, including airlines and aircraft that are now history.

The intent here is to depict essentially a dawn-to-post-dusk typical day; the ebb and flow of activity that workers at the airport experience continually. This required multiple trips to BWI to capture various aspects of the daily routine at different locations; I forced myself to make the trek numerous times—including a cold, wet day in December.

Two people merit significant mention in terms of making this possible. One is Dan Breitenbach, to whom the book is dedicated, as noted above. The other is Tony Storck, who, among other things, introduced me to Dan.

Through both their efforts, I was able to have multiple quality opportunities to capture this fascinating industry going about its daily business. I hope that you enjoy the result!

Except as noted, all photos are by George W. Hamlin.

1

By the Dawn's Early Light

By the time you stagger into the terminal for an early flight, desperate for a cup of coffee to provide some forward momentum, the airport and its inhabitants have been fully operational for some time.

Aircraft which have spent the night are readied for departure: crews arrive and stow their gear; fueling and other servicing takes place as needed; bags arrive at planeside; and, finally, bleary-eyed travelers find their gates and await the boarding process. A few will get to walk across the ramp, with at least a brief exposure to the activity there, but most will approach their transport via the ubiquitous enclosed loading bridge.

At the same time, "red-eye" flights arrive, often with bellies chock full of both bags and cargo, ready to be serviced and dispatched to join the outbound parade of morning flights. Freighters may have arrived in the pre-dawn darkness, been unloaded and readied for their daytime rest, in all but a few cases.

As the a.m. rush progresses, there are other arrivals which have originated in the morning, rather than late the previous night, having participated in the *reveille* routine at airports elsewhere. By this point, both aircraft and passengers are tuned up for the day, and ready for the activities which will occupy both until another evening's rest is in the offing, at least for the people.

At a number of locations, some of the more distinctive departures in the morning are the "sunbirds," headed for warm weather destinations such as Mexico and the Caribbean. On the beach by mid-afternoon is not a bad trade for having to be at the airport at a time more appropriate for arriving at a day job!

Finally, there may be a brief lull in the activity between the departures of the early morning wave and mid-morning arrivals from more distant destinations. It will not last long, however!

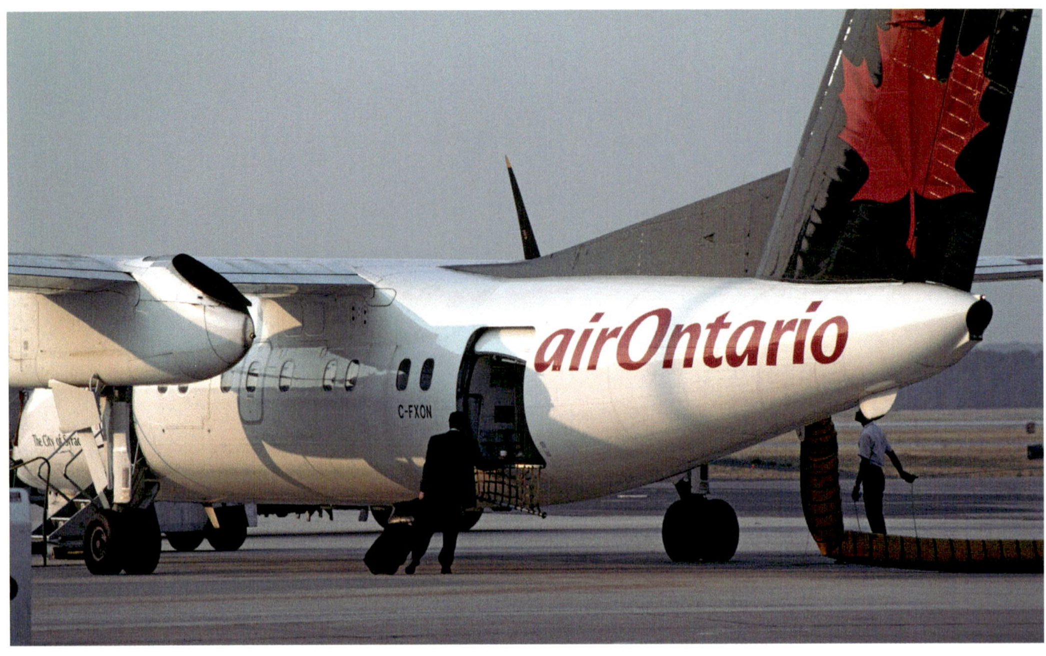

The flight attendant for Air Ontario's morning flight to Toronto, coffee cup in hand, arrives at his aircraft, and prepares to store his roll-aboard luggage in the baggage area of the aircraft. C-FXON is a de Havilland Canada DHC-8-100, commonly referred to as a "Dash 8," and is being operated as a regional/commuter service for Air Canada.

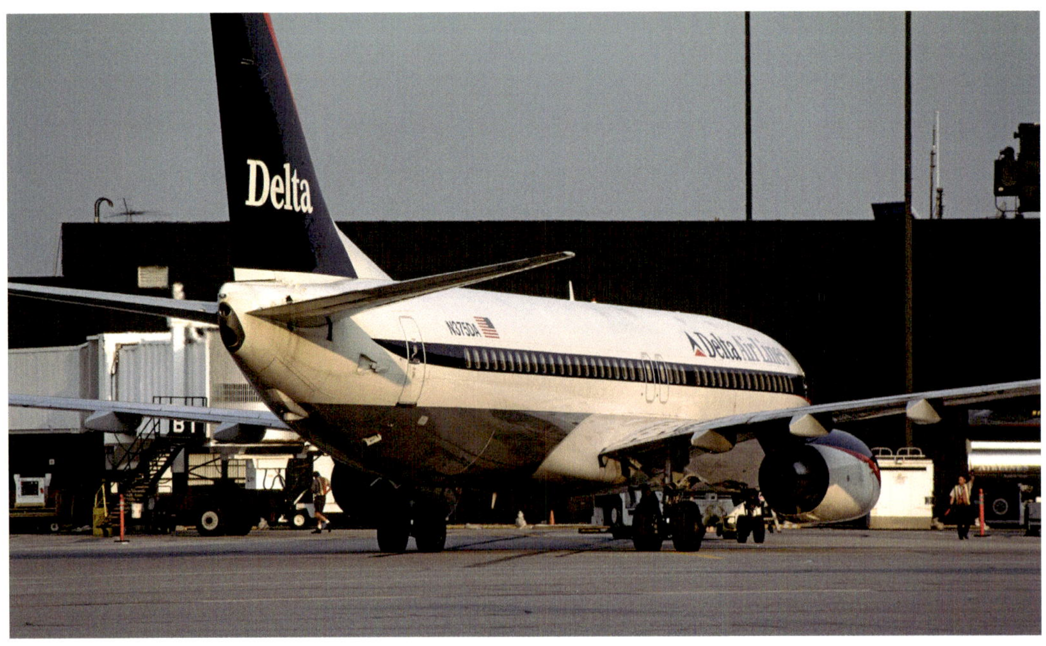

Nearby, Delta Airlines' Boeing 737-800 N375DA is being pushed back from its departure gate.

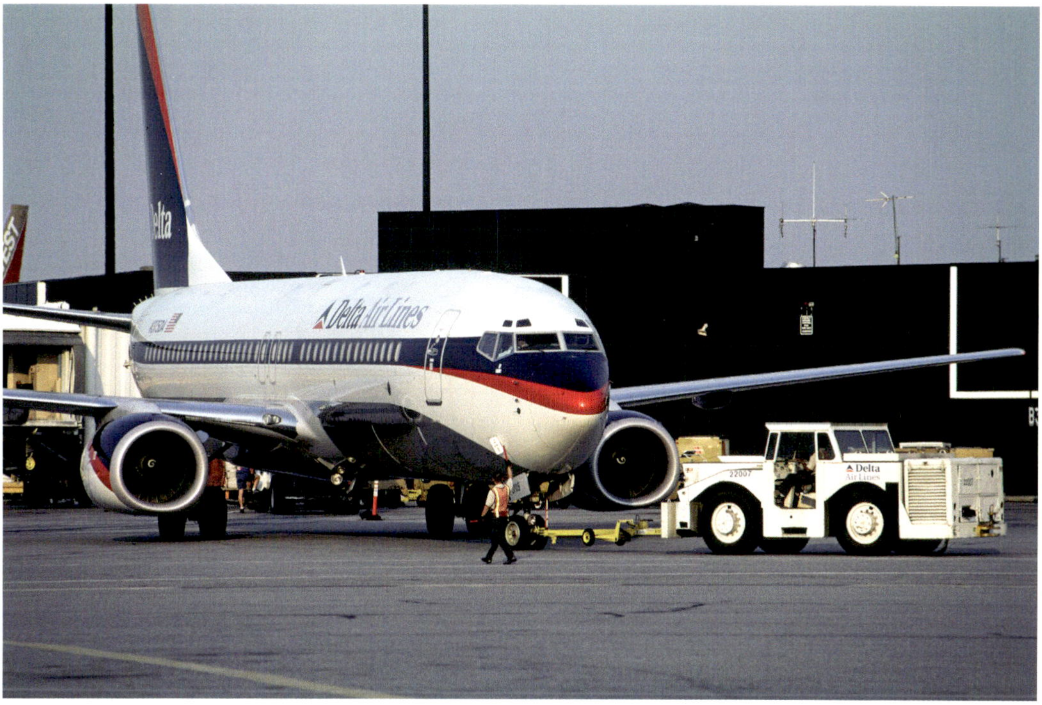

N375DA has now been turned so that it will be able to taxi away from the gate concourse and head for the departure runway once the towbar is unhooked from the nosewheel landing gear.

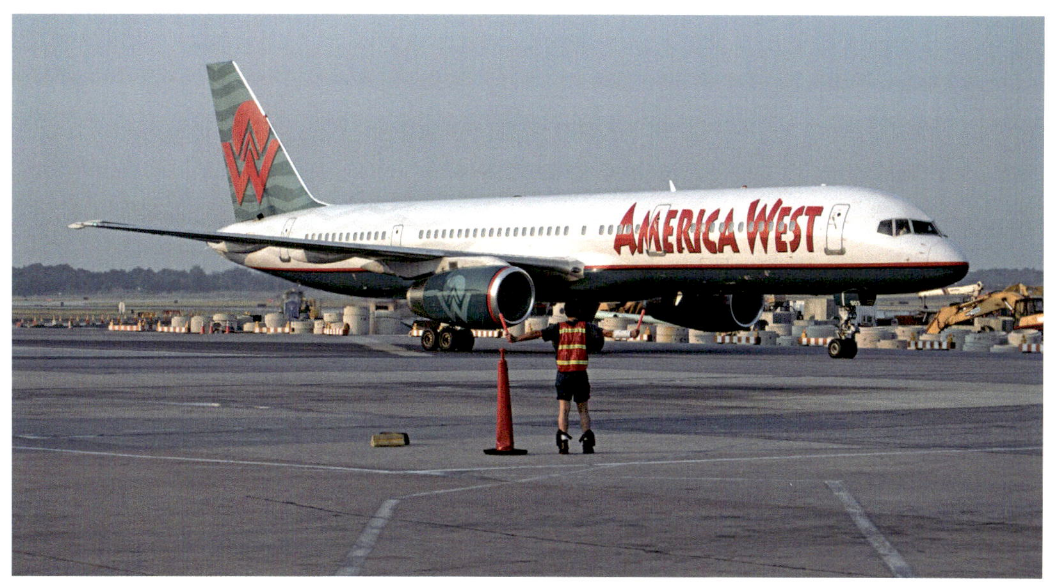

Meanwhile, at an adjacent gate, an America West Airlines Boeing 757 has arrived with an overnight "red-eye" flight (a reference to the "joys" of sitting up in an airline seat instead of sleeping in a bed) from Phoenix, Arizona, and is about to turn into its assigned gate.

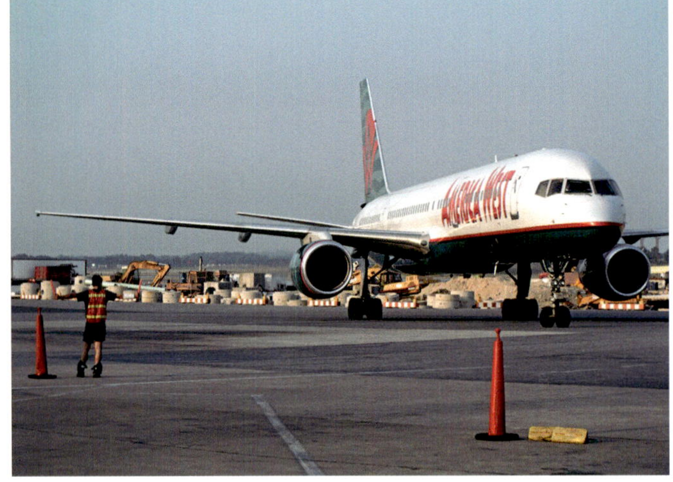

A hard turn to the right puts N903AW on a path to its parking place, with a ramp worker prepared to guide it to a proper stop.

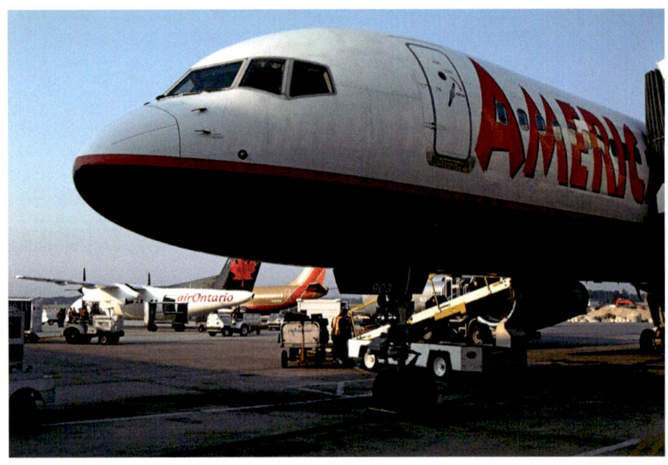

Now parked at the gate, baggage is being unloaded from the right side of N903AW, while passengers are disembarking through the loading bridge that is positioned on the "L2" (left side, second back from the nose) main entry door, a typical practice on 757s. C-FXON is positioned to the left of the America West aircraft.

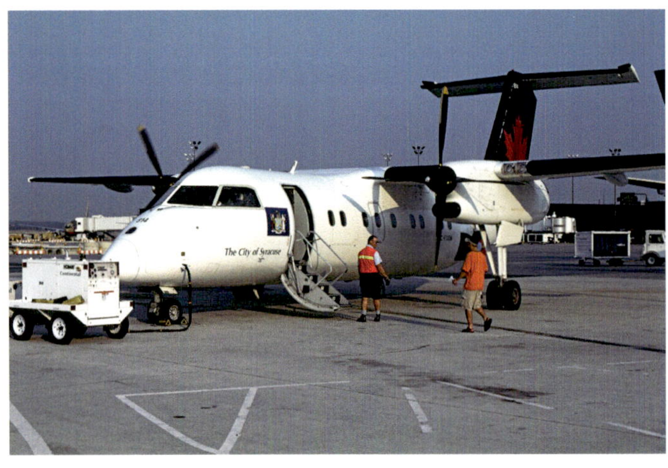

The Air Ontario Dash 8 is ready to go, once the passenger approaching boards the aircraft; the prop on the number two engine is already turning.

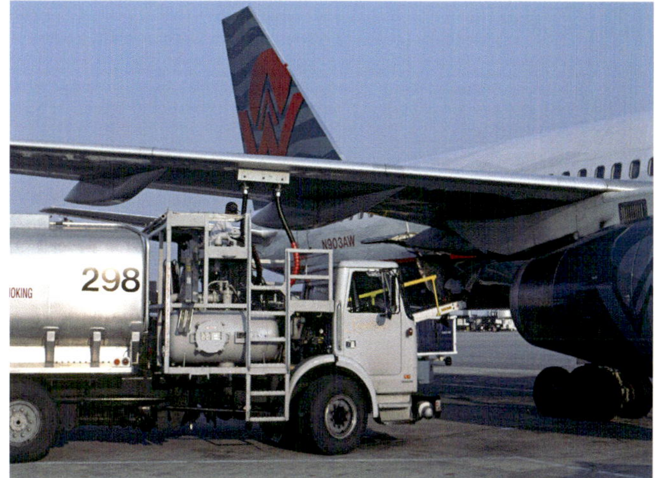

Back at the America West gate, the aircraft is in the process of being refueled for its upcoming departure. To the right of the fuel truck, a ramp worked is positioned in the aft belly pit of the 757, awaiting outgoing baggage.

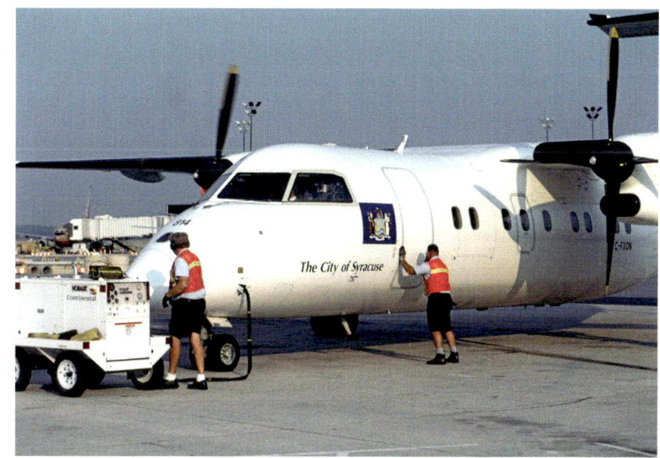

Now that C-FXON's last passenger is on board, the main entry door can be closed.

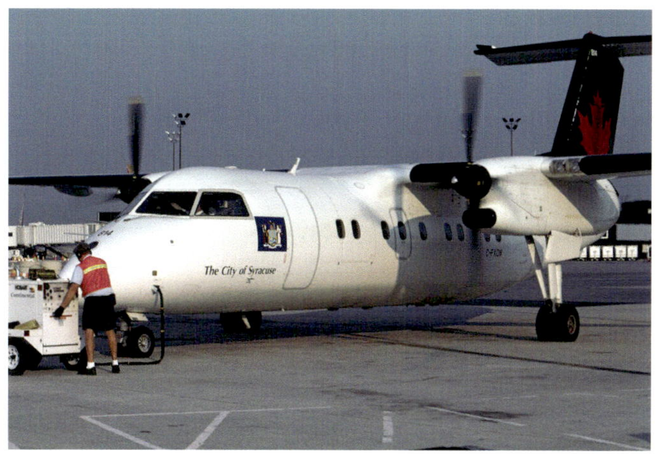

With the door shut, the left engine (number one) has now been started, so that the ground power unit can be disconnected and moved out of the way.

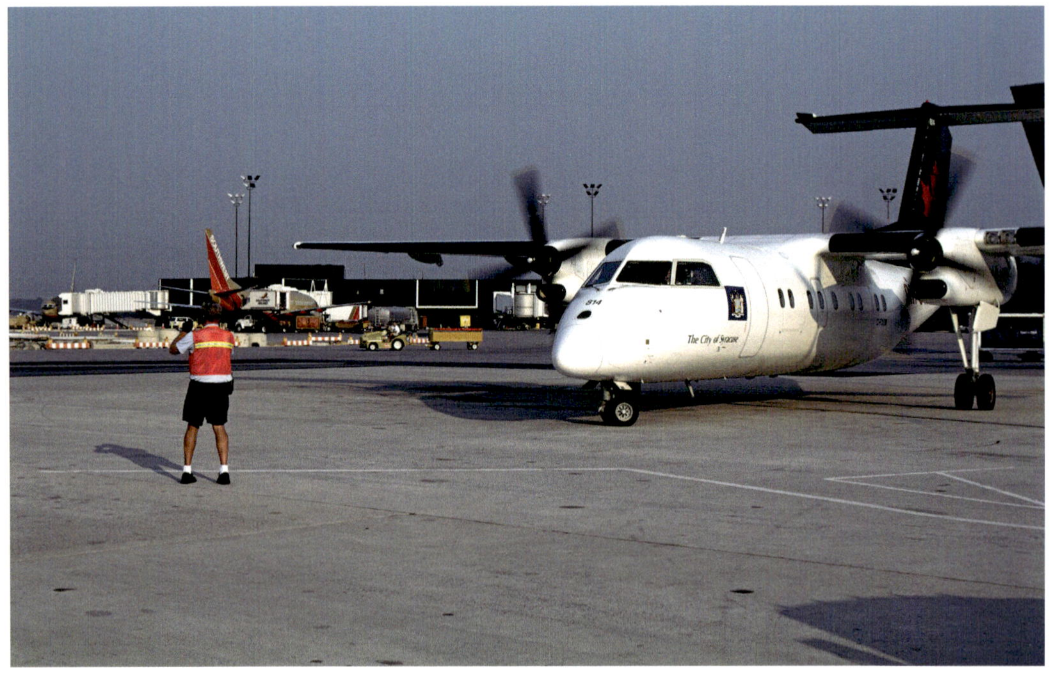

Ready to taxi, and turning away from its parking position, the Dash 8 heads for the runway.

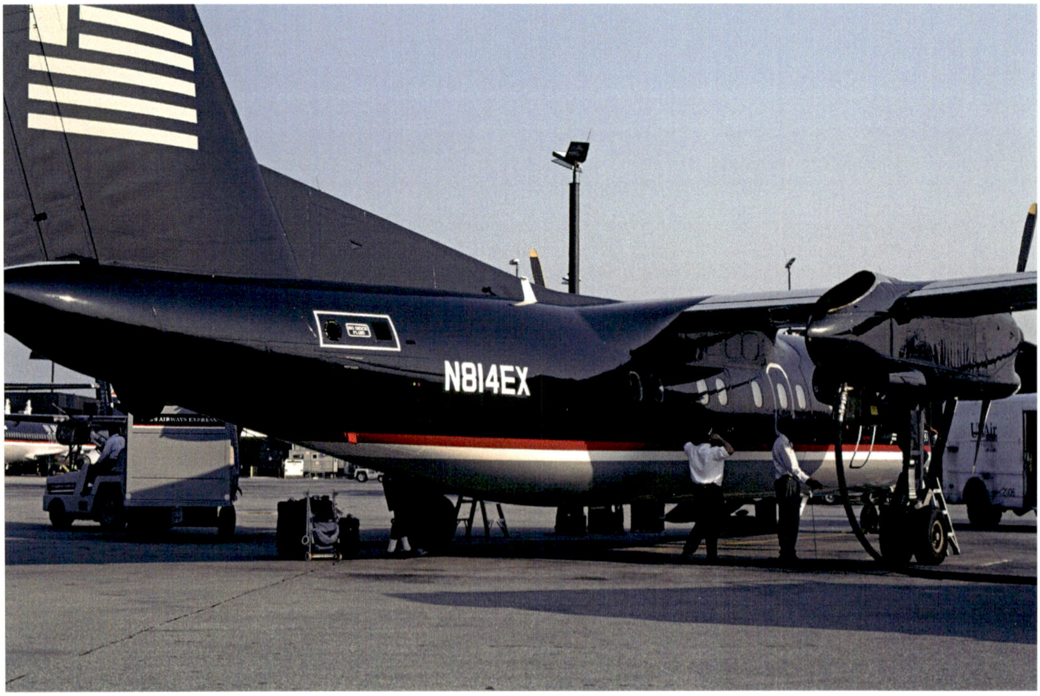

On Concourse E, a US Airways Dash 8 is being serviced, including fueling.

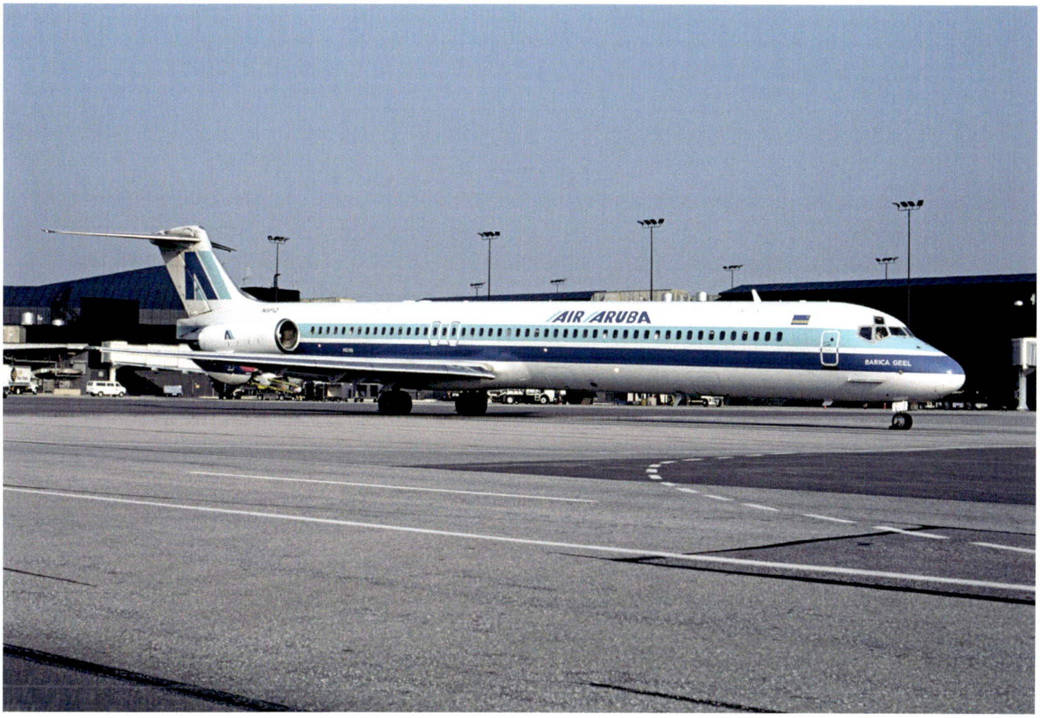

Above: Air Aruba's MD-88 N11FQ (the U.S. registration number indicating that the airline is leasing the aircraft from a financial entity domiciled in the United States) is beginning its relatively lengthy journey to near the northern coast of South America.

Right: Also on the Concourse E ramp is MD-11 N273WA of World Airways. During this time period, that airline flew a number of flights as charters for the U.S. military, using BWI Airport as a base for these operations.

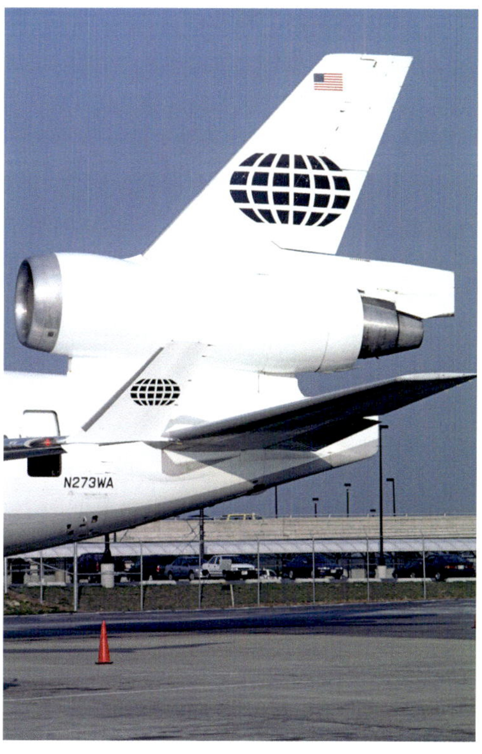

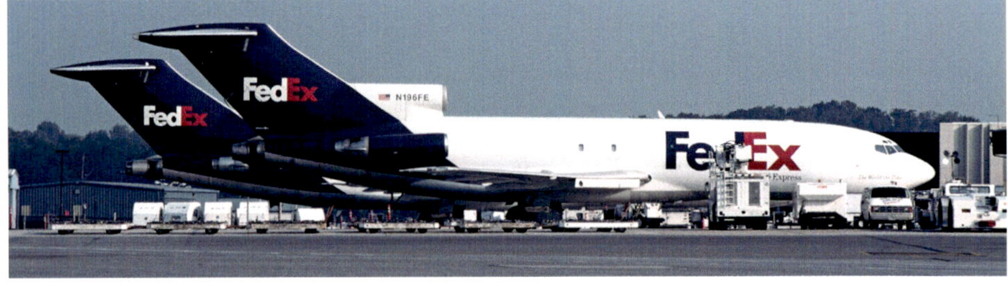

To the rear of our previous views on the E ramp is one of BWI's cargo areas, where a pair of FedEx Boeing 727s await their next assignment.

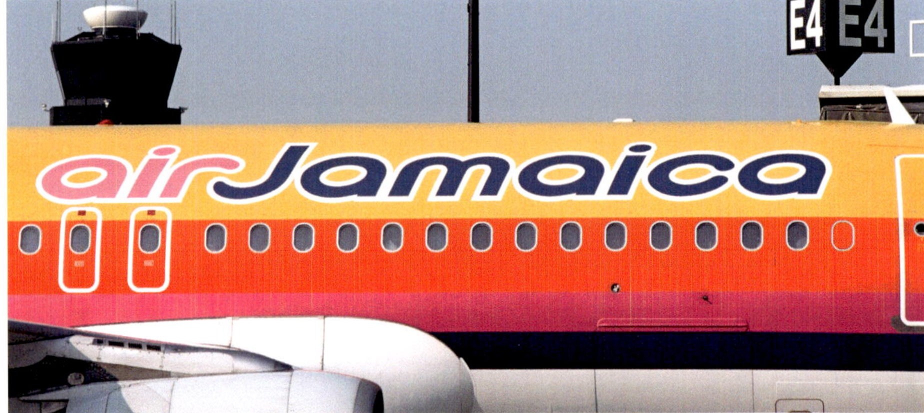

Looking again at the E concourse, Air Jamaica's colorful Airbus A320 is parked at Gate 4 and is almost ready for departure.

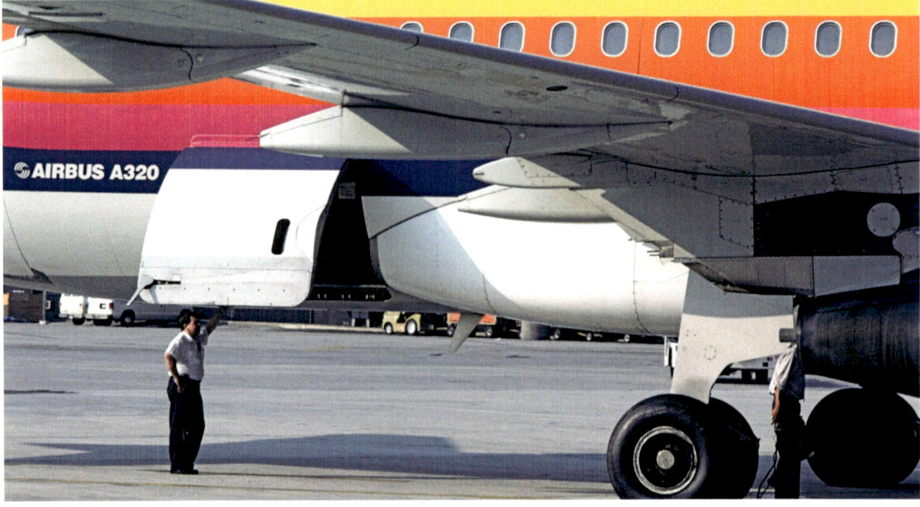

Apparently at least one more bag needs to be loaded before the Air Jamaica flight can depart; in anticipation, the rear belly pit door is almost closed.

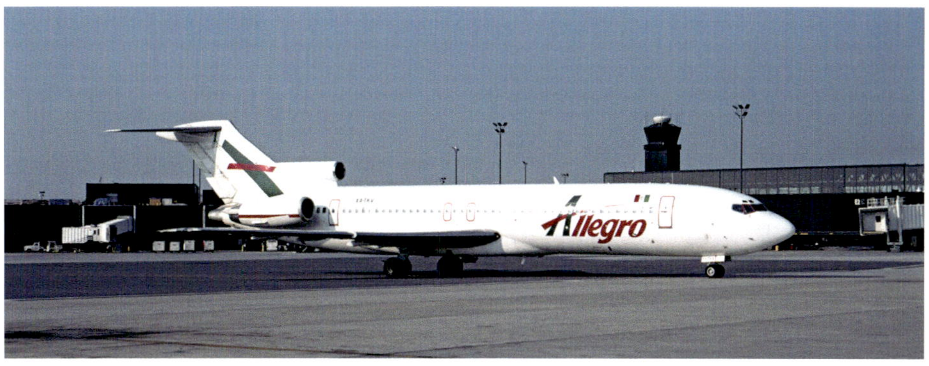

A Boeing 727-200 of Allegro Airlines, a Mexican charter and scheduled carrier, arrives, and heads for its parking gate.

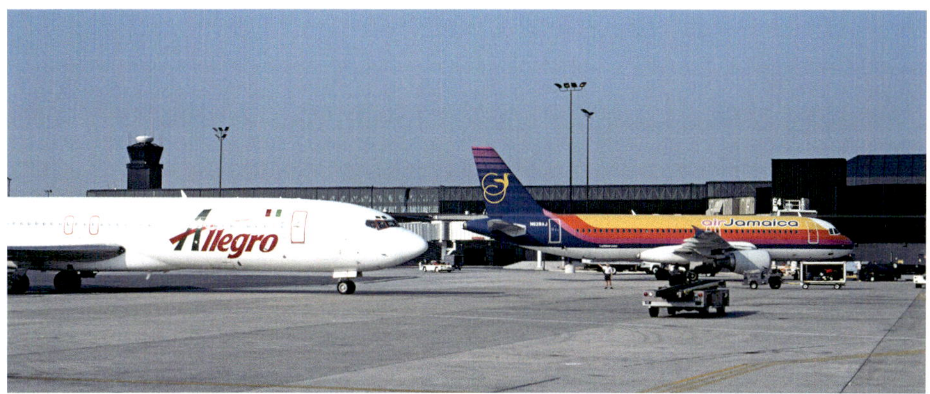

XA-TKV (the Mexican registration) heads for Gate E6, and is about to pass the Air Jamaica A320, which is still at the gate, but appears to be ready to go, with the rear belly door closed.

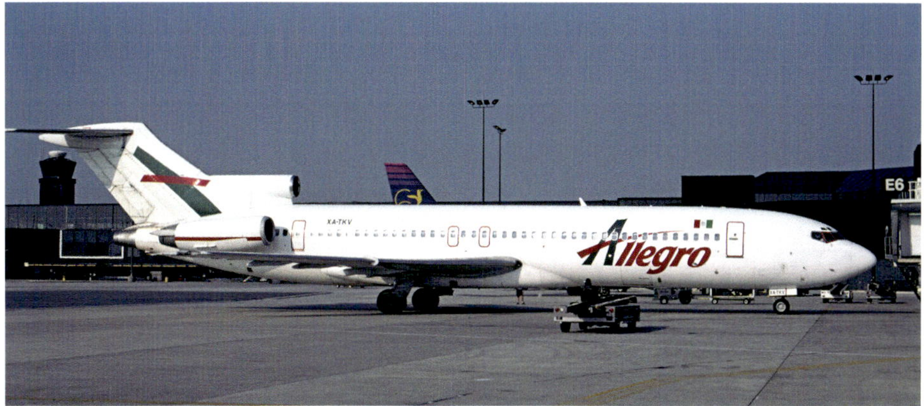

A belt loader is ready to pull up to the forward belly on "Kilo Victor" (the final two letters of its registration, a practice often used to identify individual aircraft within an airline's fleet if it is based in a country that uses an all-letter registration).

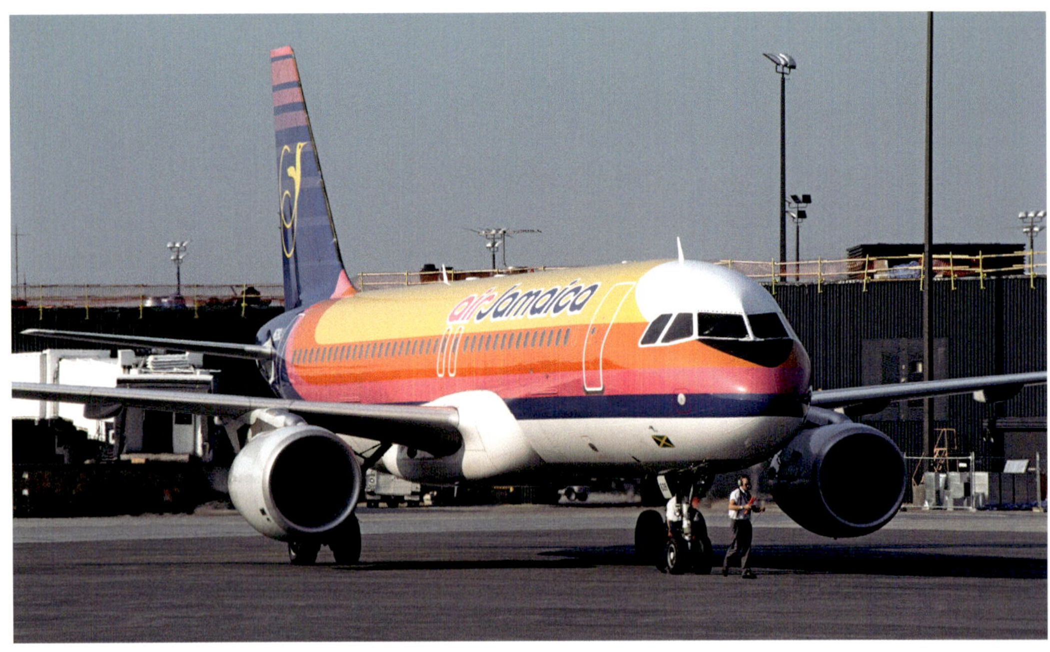

Meanwhile, the Air Jamaica A320 has been pushed back and is now ready to taxi.

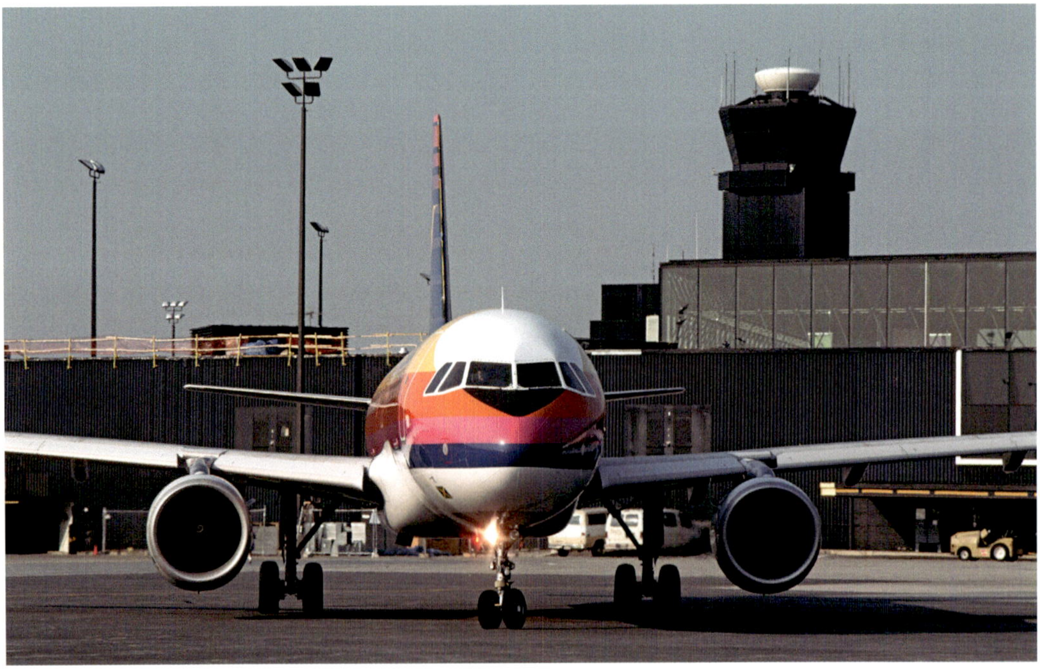

With the ramp personnel out of the way, the A320 proceeds to depart, with the BWI tower on the main terminal building as a backdrop.

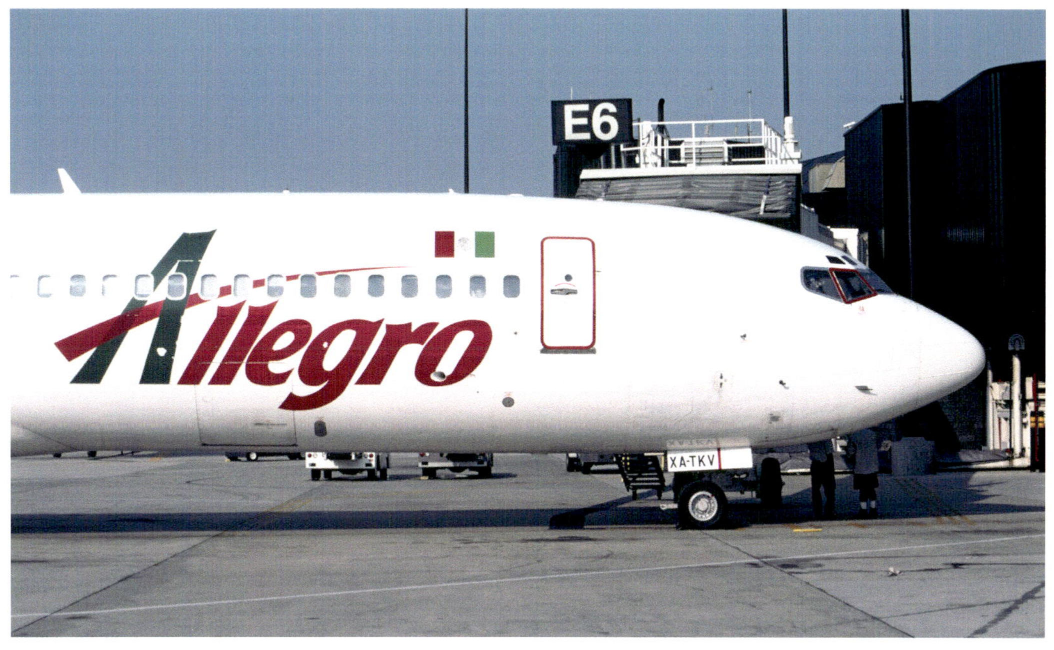

Apparently, there was not much baggage to handle on the Allegro aircraft (it likely was being positioned for loading after spending the night at a remote parking place, rather than at the gate).

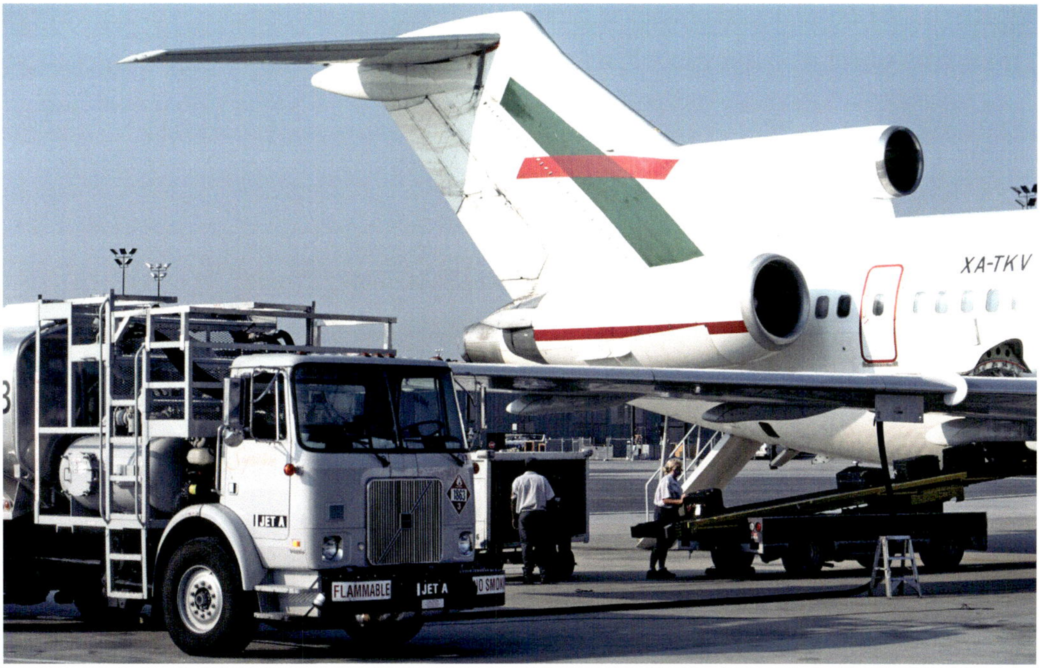

Further back, however, a fueling truck is supplying Jet A to the 727 for its upcoming trip, and baggage is being loaded into the rear belly.

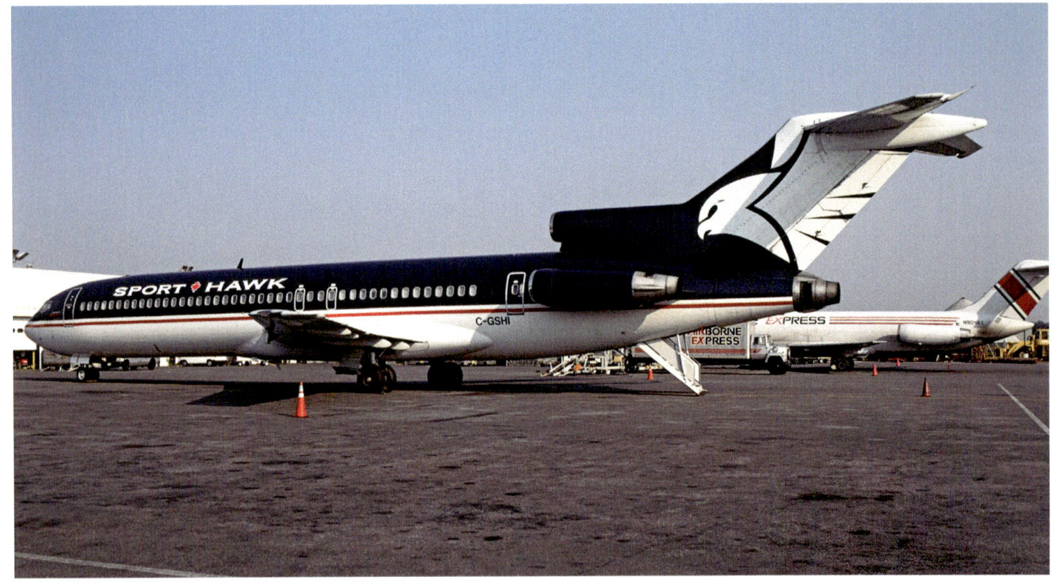

Over on the cargo ramp, a Canadian-registered 727-200 labeled with "Sport Hawk" titles operated by Skyservice airlines is parked. This aircraft began its career with TWA (Trans World Airlines), and is now operating in charter service, including flights for professional sports teams, including the Toronto Blue Jays.

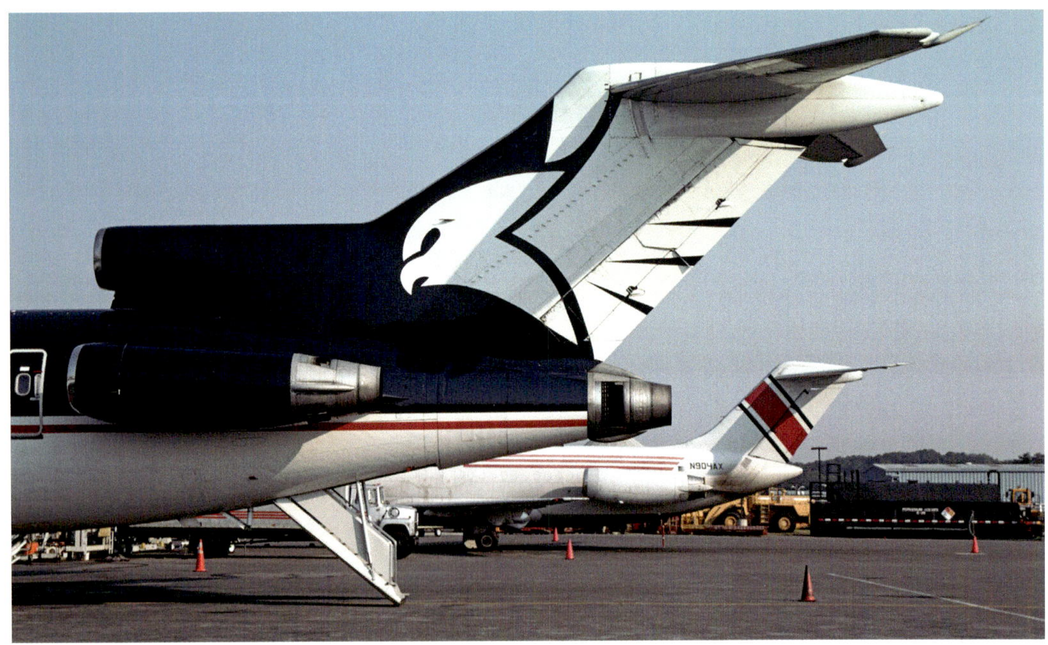

A closer look at the fierce-looking representation of a raptor on C-GSHI's tail suggests that real (avian) blue jays might have some concern with being in its vicinity. N904AX behind it is a DC-9-30 in the fleet of cargo carrier Airborne Express, based in Wilmington, Ohio.

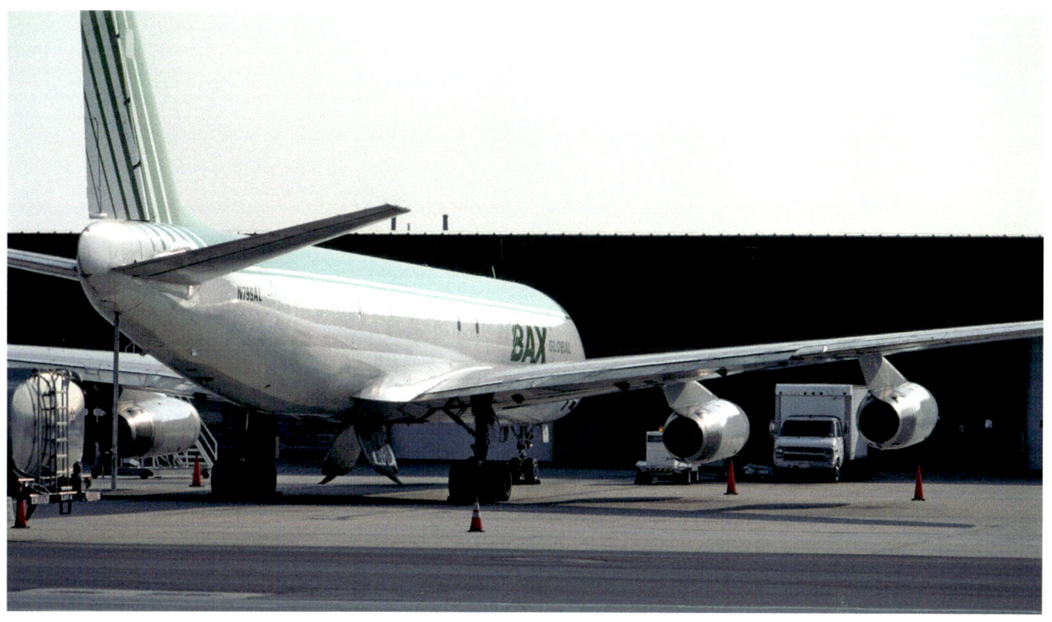

Also seen laying over on the North Cargo ramp is N799AL, a McDonnell Douglas DC-8-62 freighter aircraft in the fleet of BAX Global, formerly known as Burlington Air Express, hence the acronym.

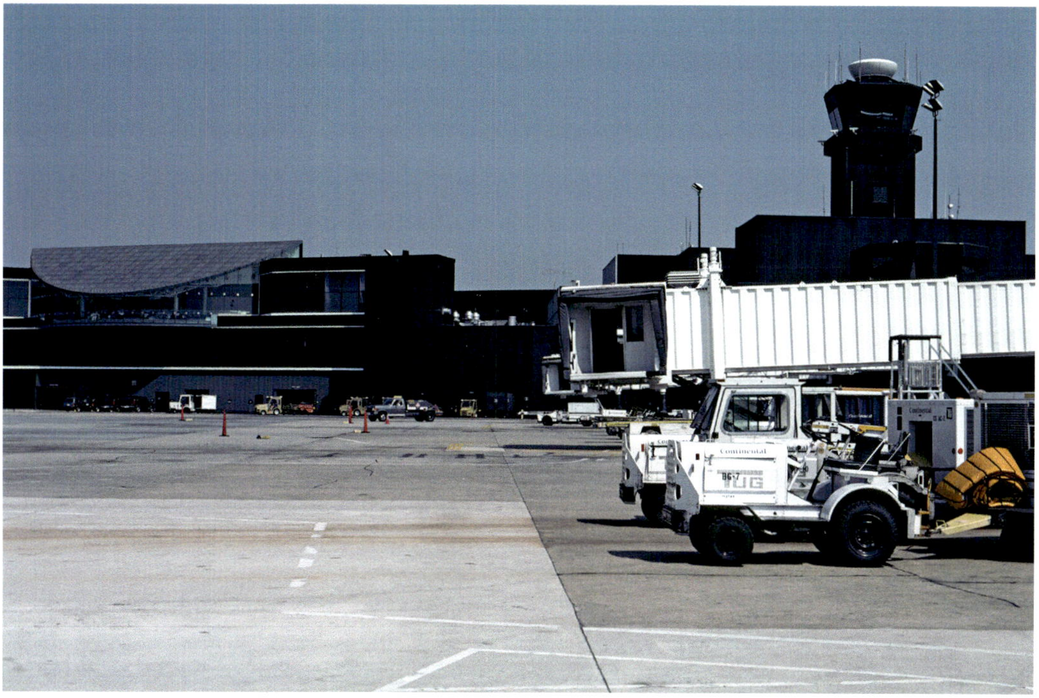

Finally, the morning rush is over, and the airport and its workers get a breather!

2

Our Cause It is Just

Once the morning peak has come and gone, routine activities take hold, and are repeated numerous times. Aircraft arrive from a variety of destinations, each one generating a crowded choreography of servicing activities as it is turned into another departure. All of this takes place in a necessarily short period of time, as the aircraft are multi-million-dollar assets, and cannot be allowed to loaf during their peak earning periods.

What might appear to border on chaos from the perspective of a terminal window is, in reality, an exercise in planning, skill, and teamwork, plus a fair amount of physical exertion, in many cases. Most aircraft require some combination of baggage and cargo handling, fueling, catering, and lavatory servicing in addition to facilitating the access of passengers from and to the aircraft. Most of the ramp action takes place on the opposite side from the passenger boarding doors, making for crowded conditions for those tasked with doing the work.

Repeatedly, the routine on the ramp is played out: arrival; loads off; replenishment of supplies; loads on; pushback; and, finally, permission to taxi, after the people on the airside teams have done their jobs. Occasionally, the scenario is complicated by the need for some non-routine maintenance, which, often, is accomplished during the relatively short periods allocated to aircraft on the ground during the operating day.

On the cargo ramp, however, the situation is reversed. Most of the freighters, unladen from their nightly burdens, are working on their suntans if it's a sunny day, awaiting another turn of frenetic activity after the sun has set. This is also the time when maintenance gets its chance to work on the cargo birds. As a result, freighter mechanics often have more desirable shift start times than their passenger industry counterparts!

One of the nuances of airline operations is that they continue "rain or shine," and in many locations, also when cold winds blow and the precipitation is solid and opaque, rather than liquid and transparent. Bags still have to be loaded and unloaded; aircraft fueled and given pre-flight walkarounds by the flight crews even while the passengers relax upstairs in climate-controlled comfort.

Rain gear helps, but after a whole shift full of wind and water, only the lucky go home dry. Aircraft ramps also accumulate an amazing number of small lakes, considering that they are inherently flat surfaces. This creates water hazards for feet, as well as the raw material for newly lit engines to geyser as aircraft taxi away.

On this sort of day, shortly after concluding that all the waterfowl (which are supposed to be designed for this) in the vicinity are in sheltered locations, an apparition arrives, in the form of an airborne whale. No problem—get it turned and on its way again, and maybe then there will be time for a break.

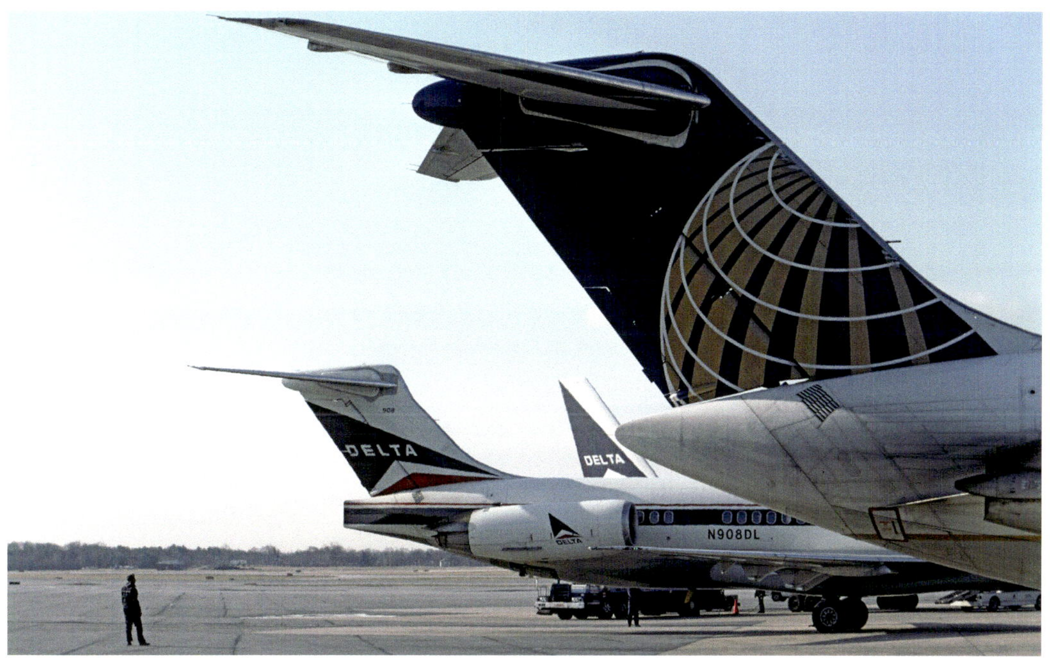

A pair of McDonnell Douglas products, a Continental DC-9, and Delta MD-88, as well as a Boeing 757, also from Delta, are at their gates here.

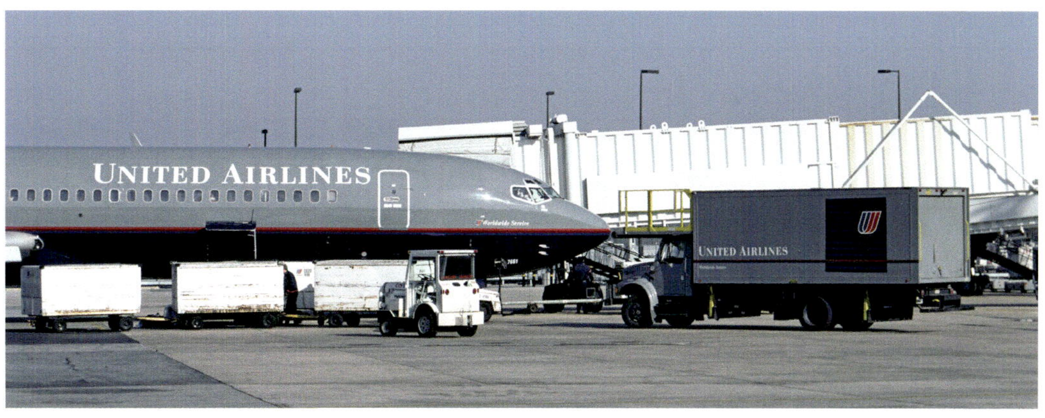

United's 727-200, N7261U, will be ready to depart shortly.

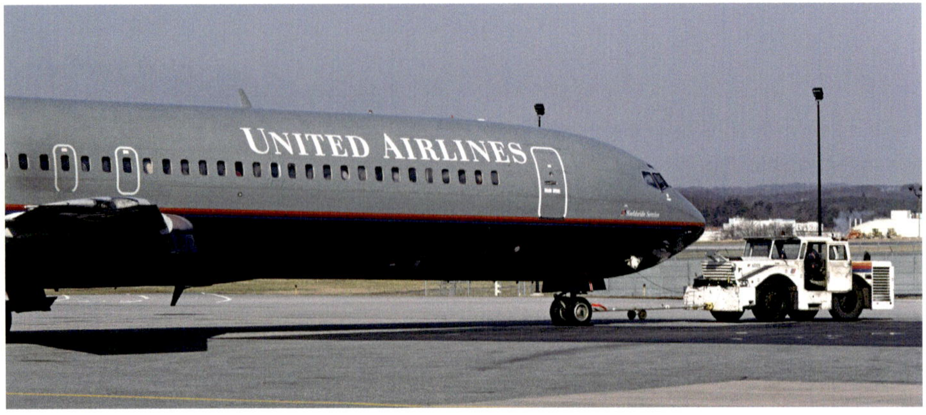

Pushback is complete, and it is time for the towbar to be removed.

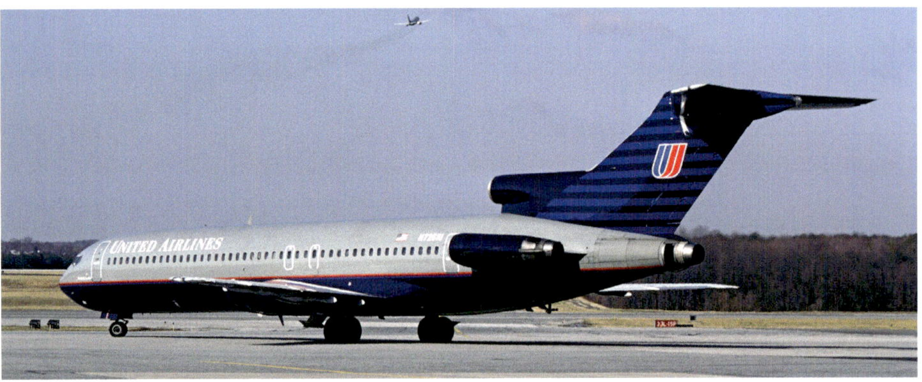

Now N7261U is taxiing for takeoff, as another aircraft climbs out after departing BWI on runway 28.

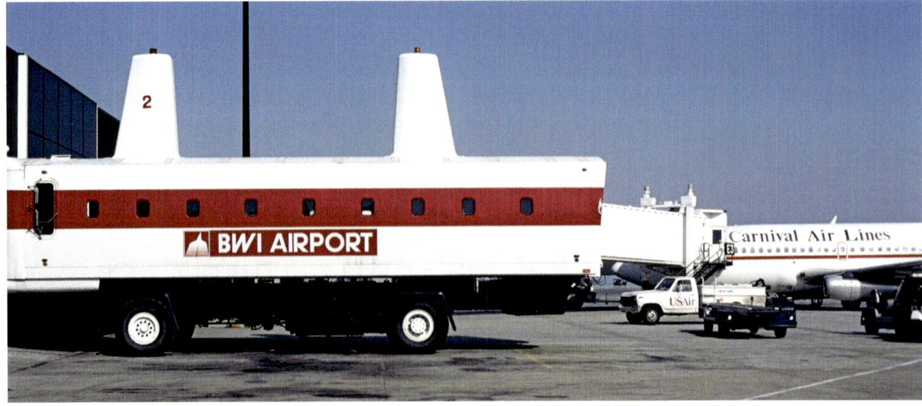

In addition to passenger loading bridges, BWI also had a pair of "Plane Mates" to get passengers to and from aircraft at remote (not at a gate on one of the concourses) parking locations.

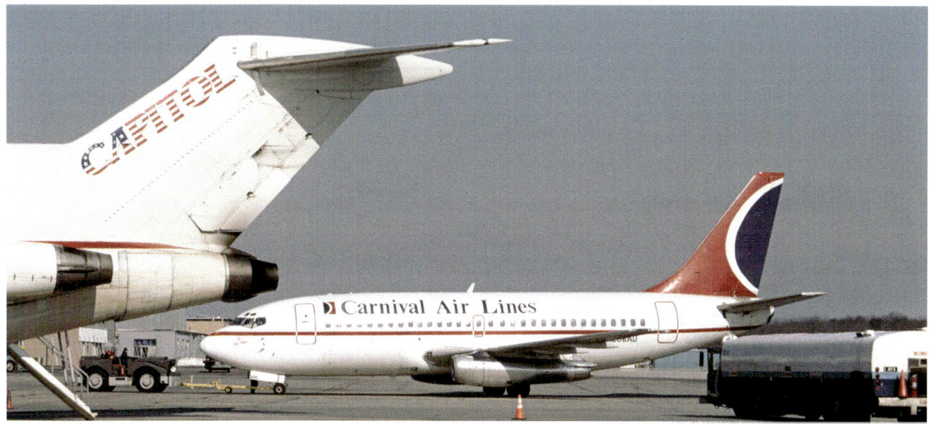

A pair of aircraft from carriers serving markets that were largely oriented towards "leisure" travelers, as opposed to business, in this case a Capitol 727, and a Carnival 737-200.

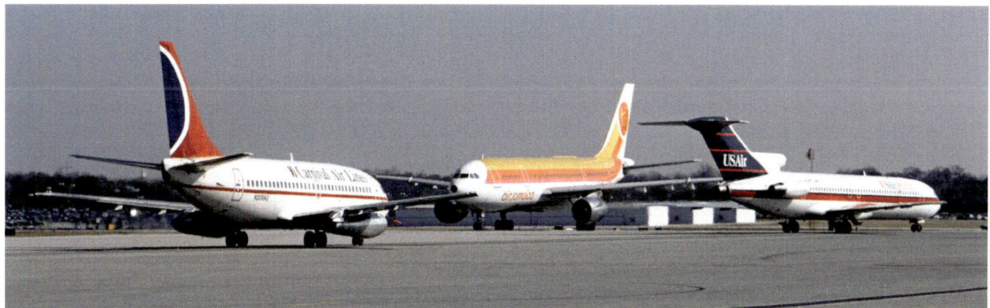

Faceoff between Carnival's 737 and Air Jamaica's Airbus A300B! At the right, a relatively unusual visitor, in terms of a USAir 727-200 from that carrier's Northeast Air Shuttle fleet; on weekends during the mid-1990s, that airline used these aircraft for leisure markets, since demand for the business travel that these aircraft catered to on weekdays was considerably lower, particularly on Saturdays, than it was during the work week.

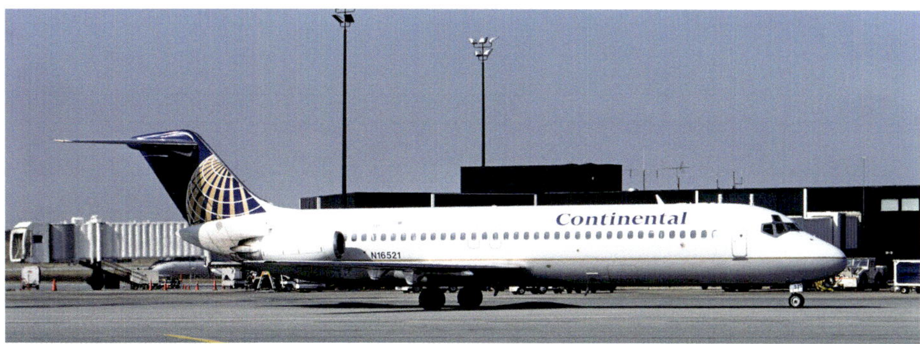

This Continental DC-9-30 is ready to go.

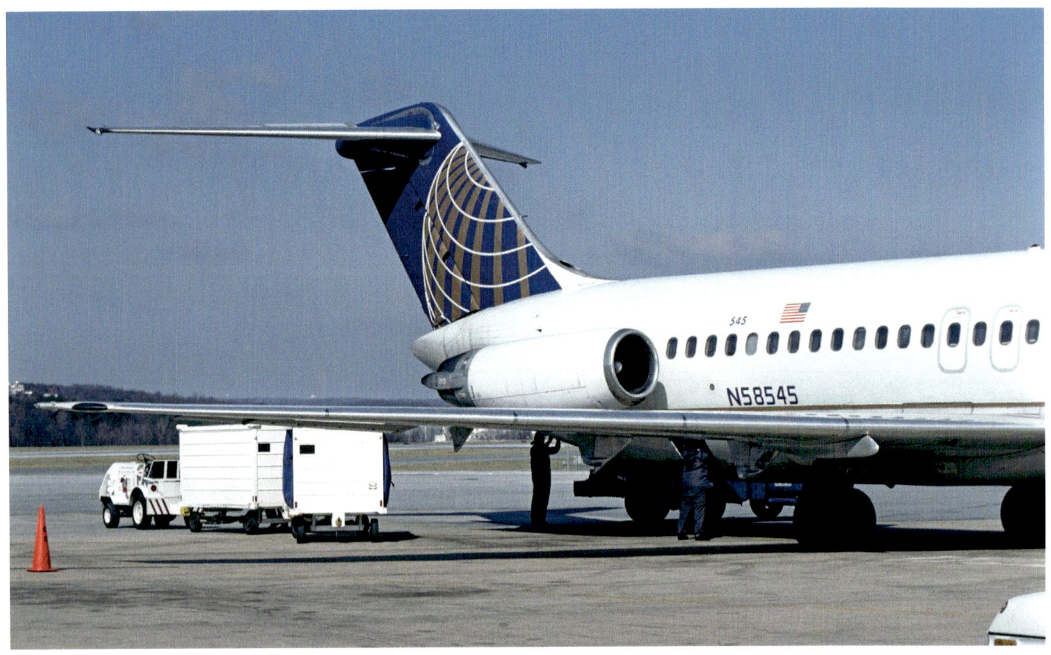

Another bag arriving planeside, after which this Continental DC-9 will join its compatriot in the departure queue.

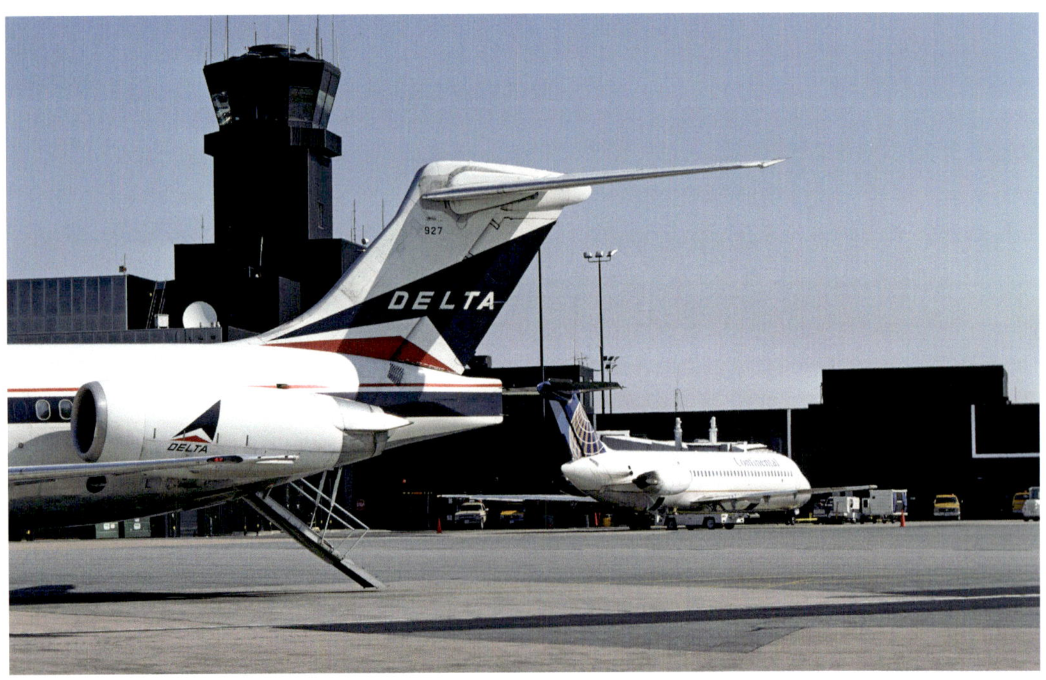

A Delta MD-88 with its ventral stairs deployed is at the next concourse over from the Continental DC-9.

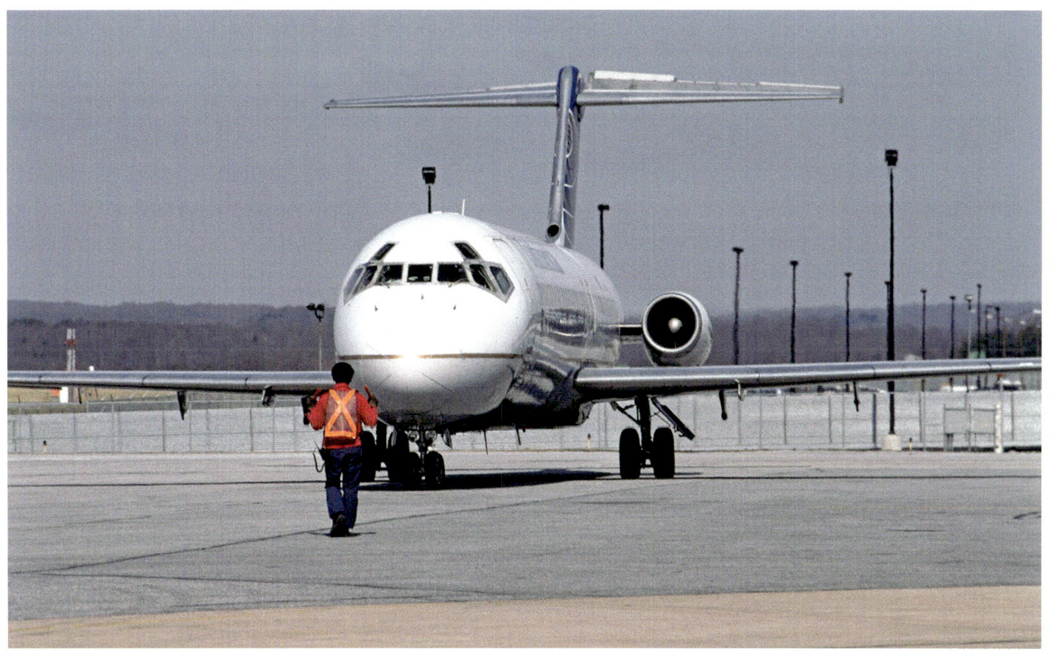

Now N58545 is ready to taxi and is being signaled to proceed.

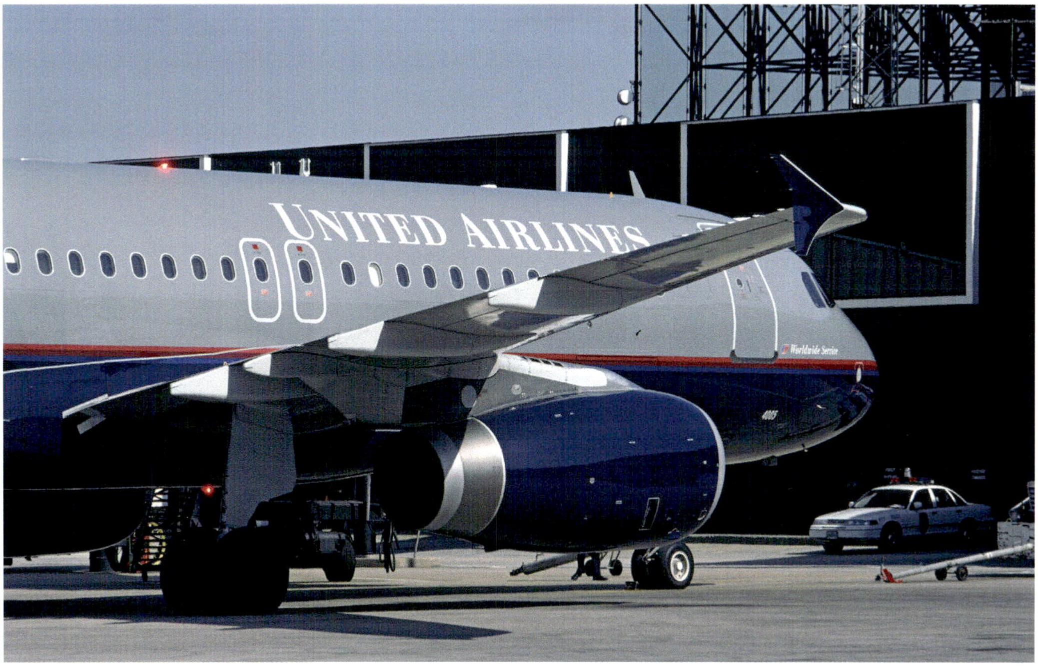

N405UA, a United A320, has just arrived at the gate, with its marker beacon still illuminated.

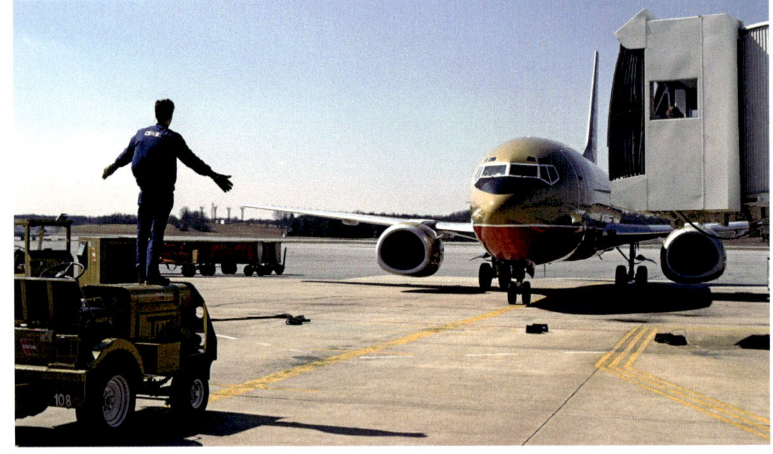

An inbound Southwest 737-500, N515SW, is being guided to its parking place at the gate.

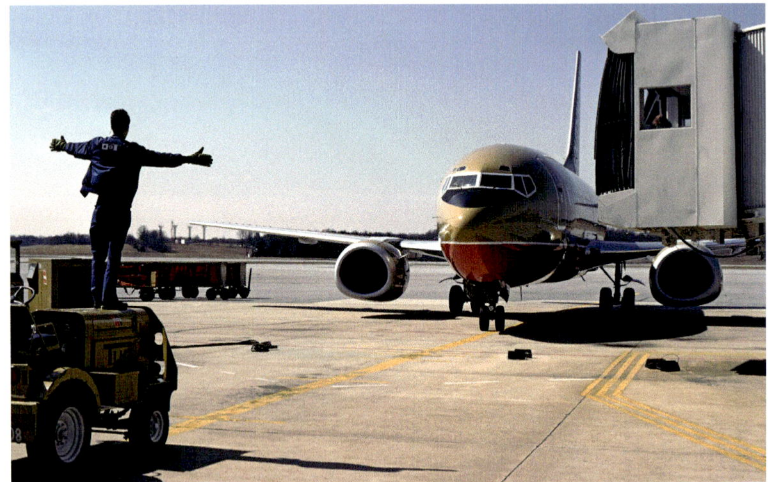

Slower...

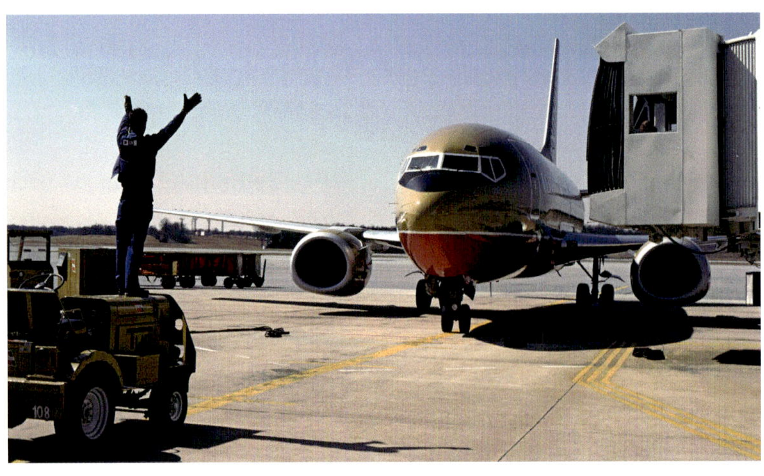

Slower...

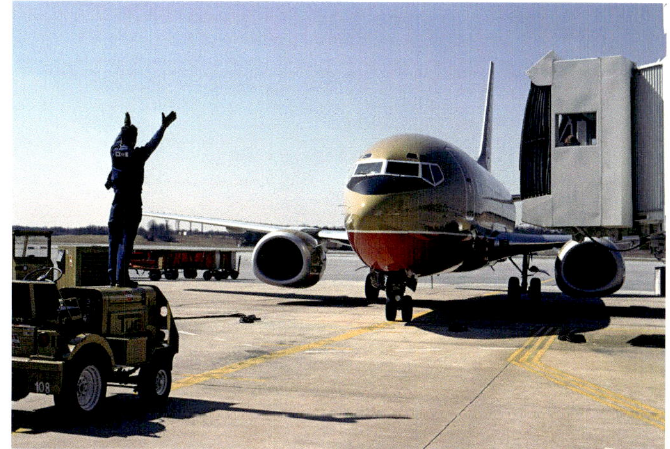

Almost there...

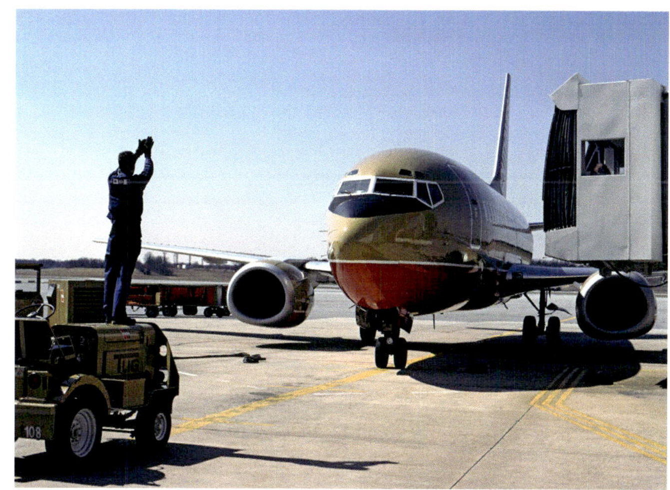

That's good!

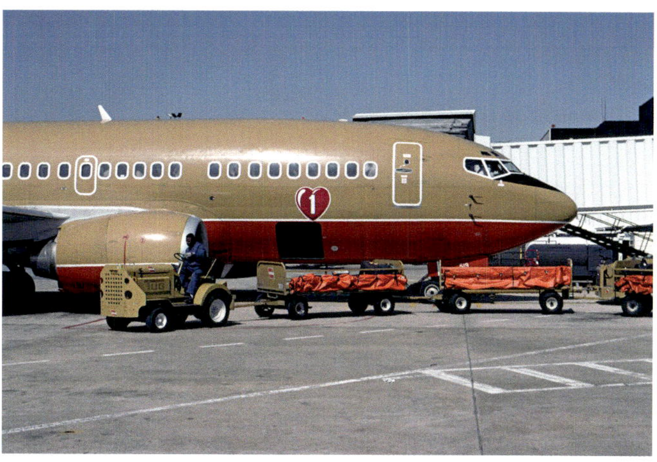

Another Southwest 737-500, N519SW, is at the adjacent gate.

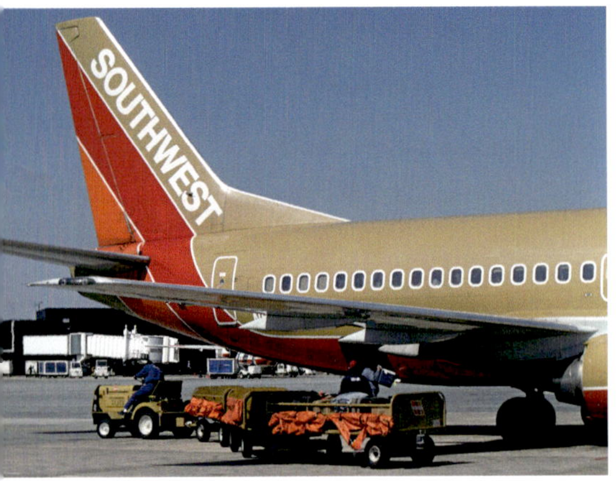

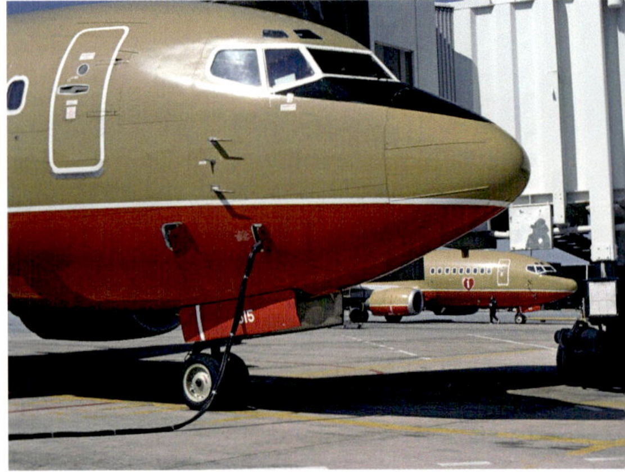

Above left: A few more bags for N519SW arrive planeside.

Above right: A look at both of the Southwest 737-500s; ground power has been hooked up to N515SW; N519SW has the towbar attached and is ready to be pushed back from the gate.

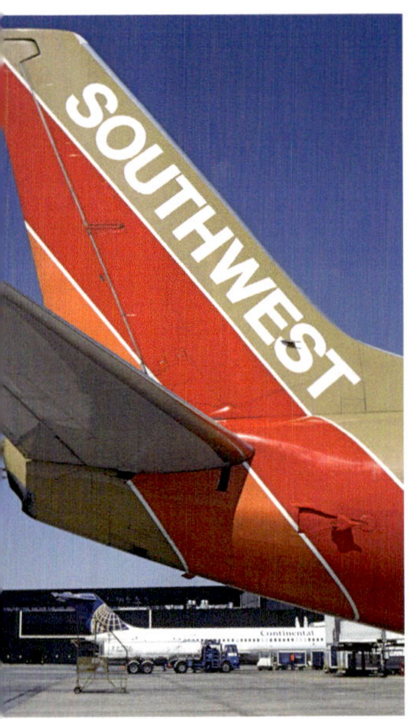

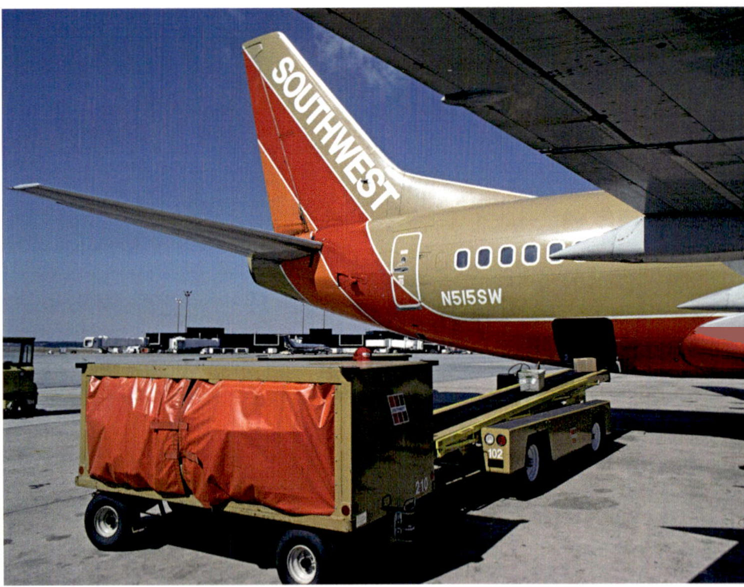

Above left: Looking down Concourse C from N515SW, another Continental DC-9 is at a gate closer to the terminal.

Above right: A few more items remain to be unloaded from N515SW.

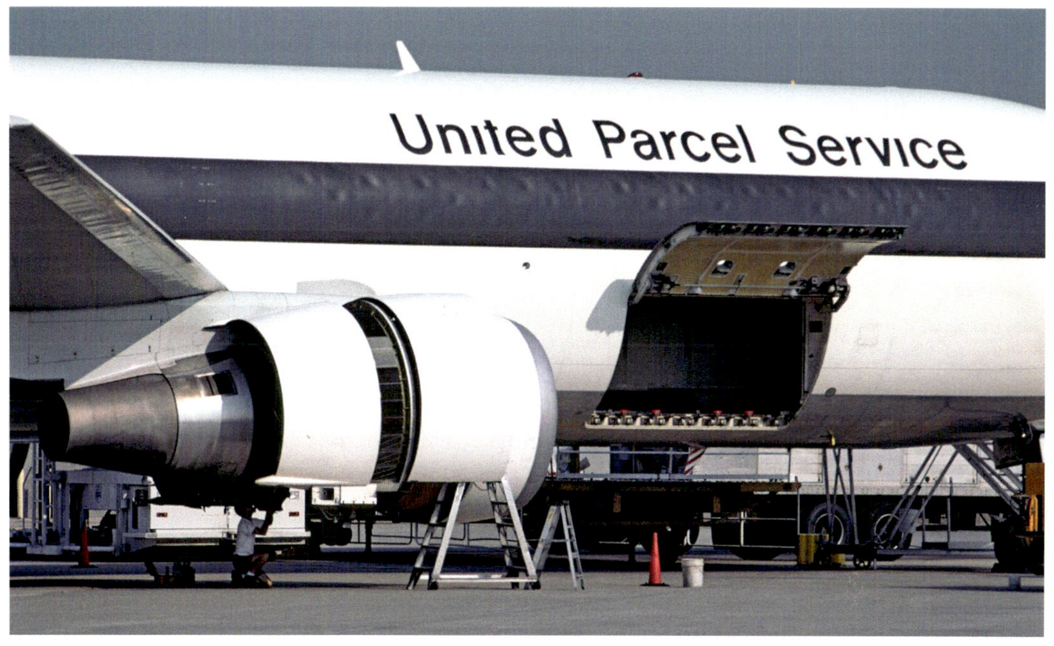

As indicated in the introduction to this chapter, maintenance on cargo aircraft is often performed during daytime layovers. Here, a UPS 767-300 freighter's number two engine is getting some attention.

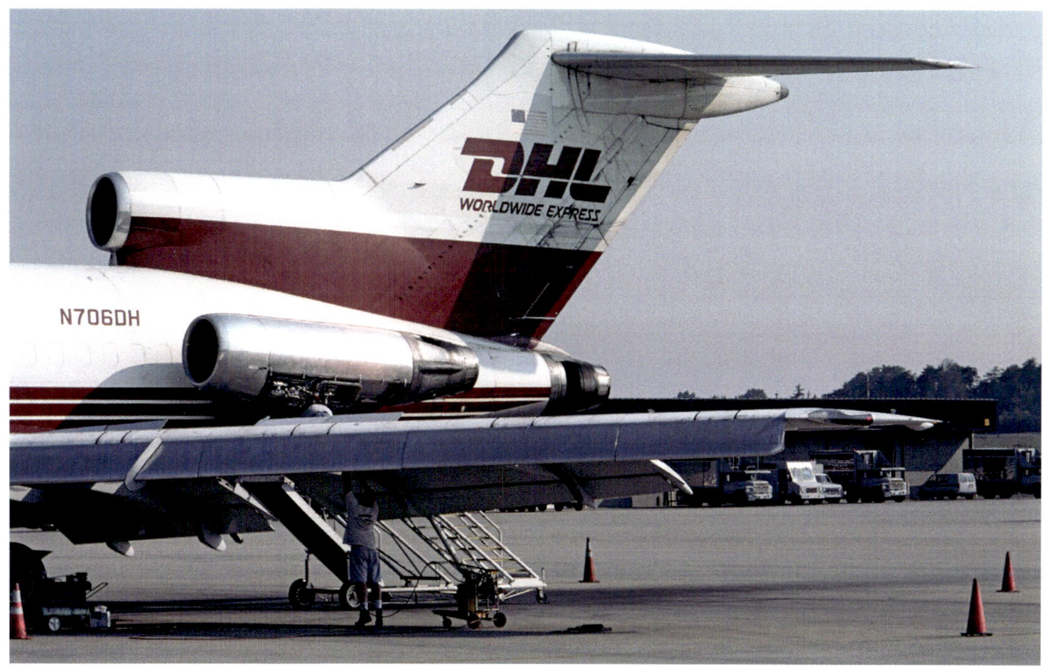

DHL's 727-100 freighter N706DH, which began its career in passenger service for United Airlines, is having its portside (number one) powerplant worked on.

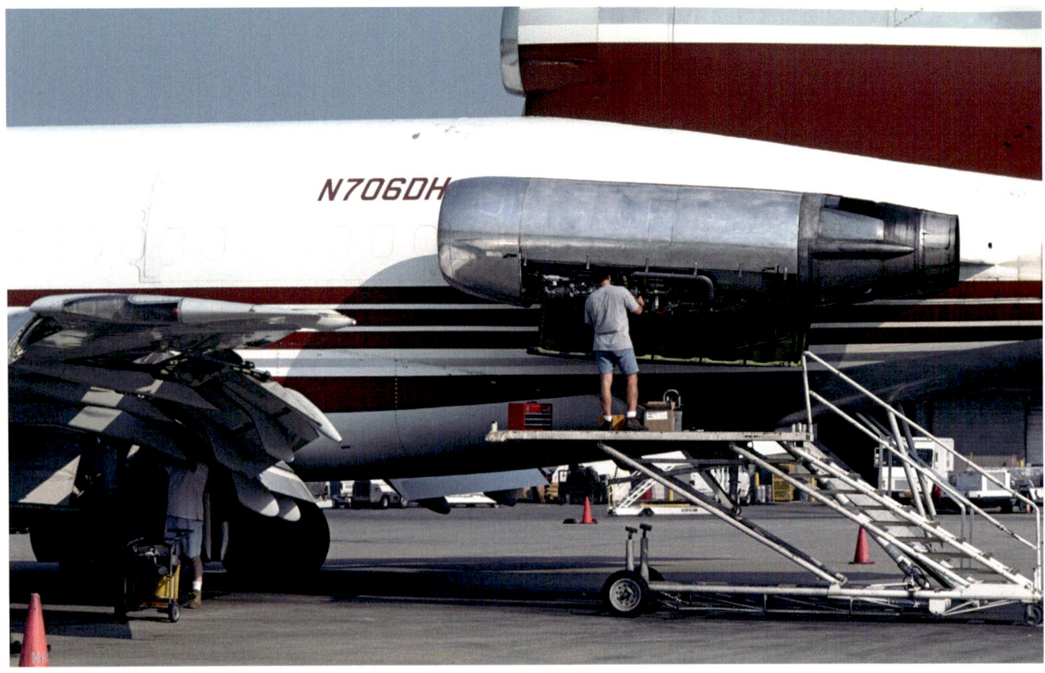

Here is a closer look at what is going on with the engine maintenance on N706DH.

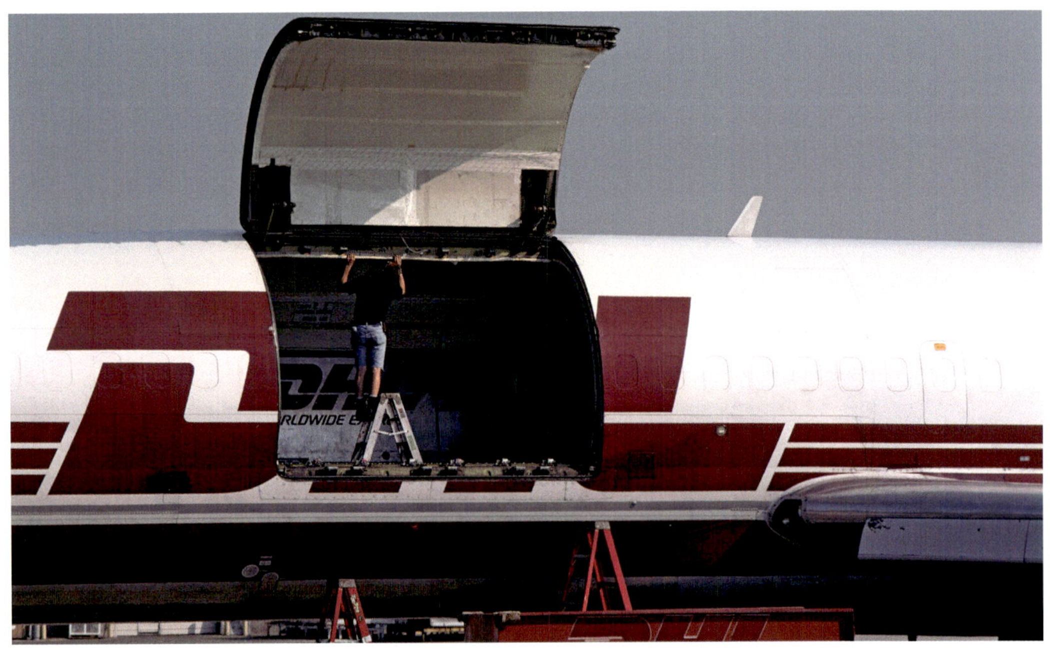

Further forward along the fuselage of the same aircraft, the main cargo door is getting a close inspection. Looking into the interior of the aircraft indicates how this space is divided up into "positions," with each one having a maximum weight limitation.

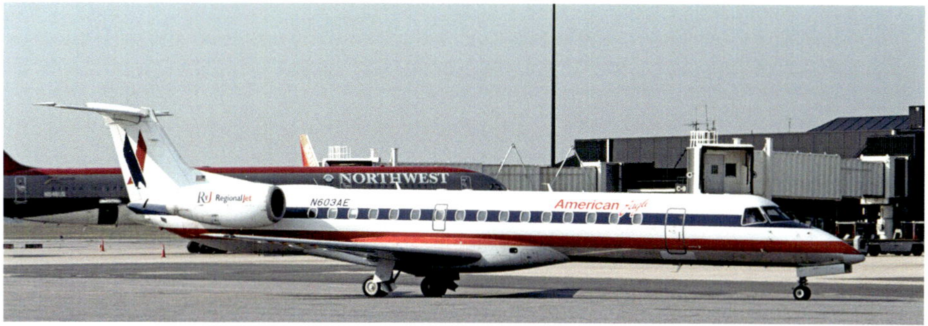

Turning back towards the nearby passenger concourse, we see American Eagle's Embraer Regional Jet EMB-145 taxiing by. Eagle is the subsidiary of American Airlines that operated most of the larger carrier's regional/feeder services at this time.

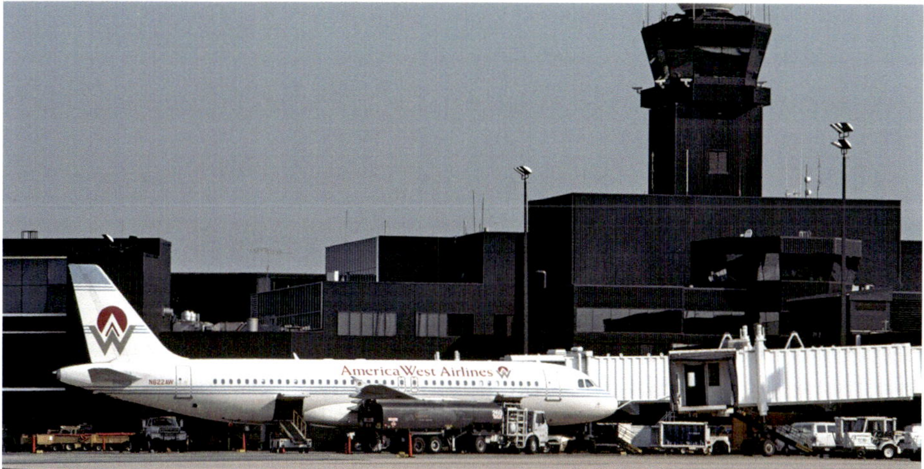

America West's A320 N622AW is being refueled while sitting at its gate on Concourse C. The aircraft is still in the airline's original colors, unlike the 757 that we saw arriving at BWI earlier.

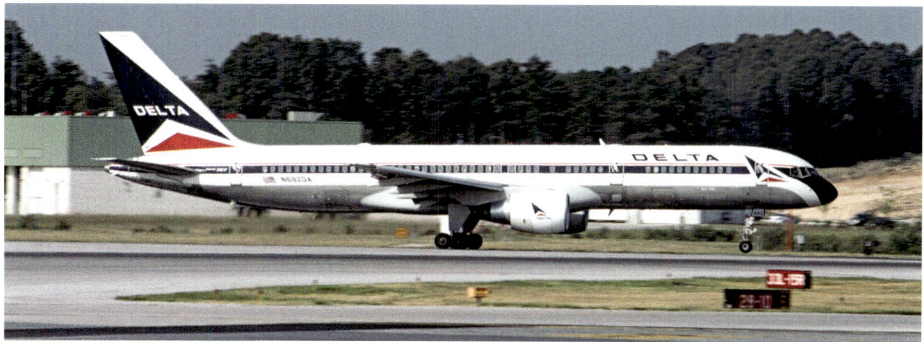

A Delta 757, N682DA, one of that airline's large fleet of the type, is accelerating on runway 33L; rotation has begun, as is evident by the nose landing gear no longer being on the pavement.

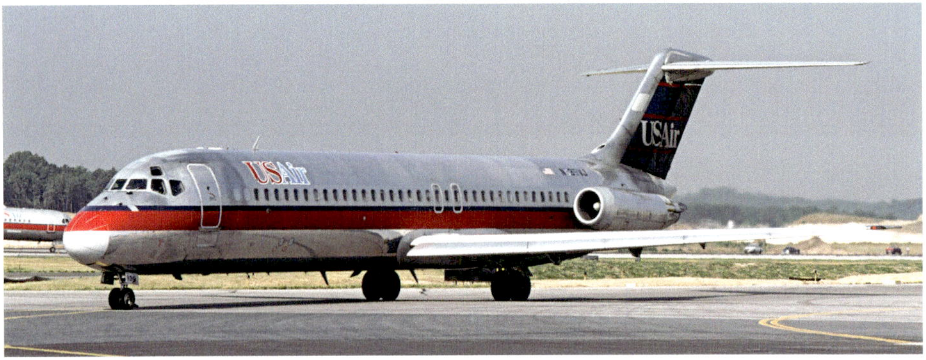

A pair of USAir aircraft, including DC-9-30 N939VJ, as well as a Fokker 100 at the far left, are taxiing on the ramp. The airline's predecessor, Allegheny, ordered seventy-five of this model of the DC-9, which is seen here in what is termed a "bare metal" paint scheme.

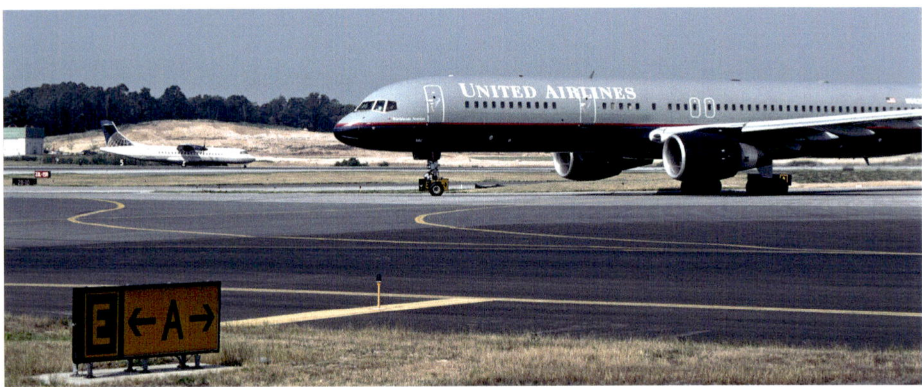

We will take a better look at that ATR-72 of Continental Express that is arriving on 33 Left in a moment; closer to the camera is a United 757 departing from BWI, and heading for the runway it will use for takeoff.

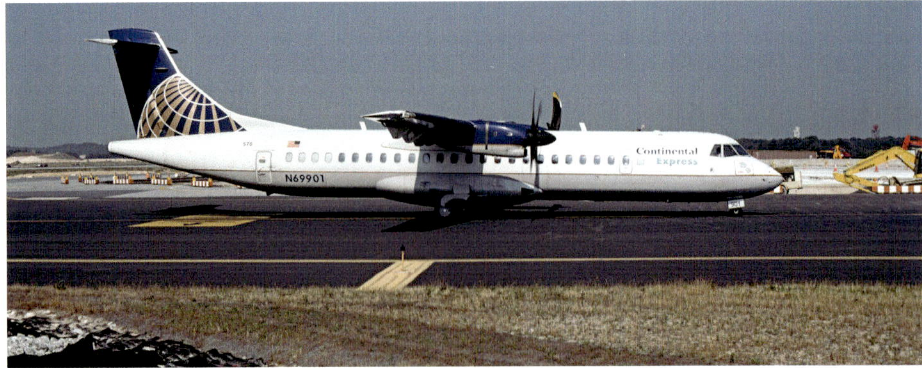

Now N69901 is ready for its closeup. This relatively high-capacity regional turboprop aircraft accommodates sixty-four passengers in its Continental Express configuration.

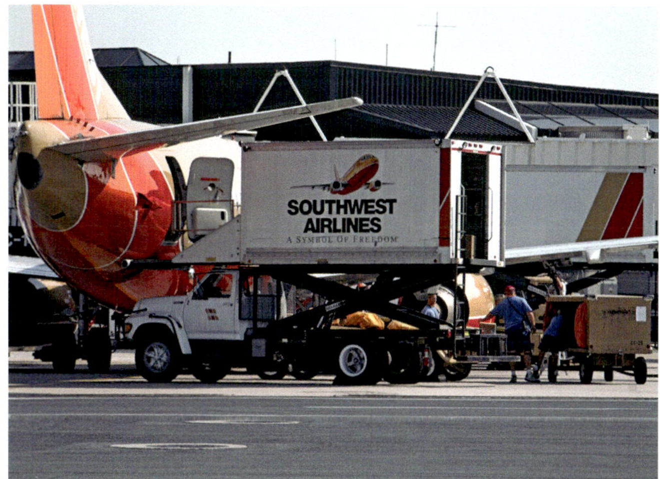

Lots of activity on a Southwest 737 at its gate, with a high-lift truck catering to the rear galley of the aircraft, while baggage is being dealt with at the rear belly, and fueling is going on under the wing.

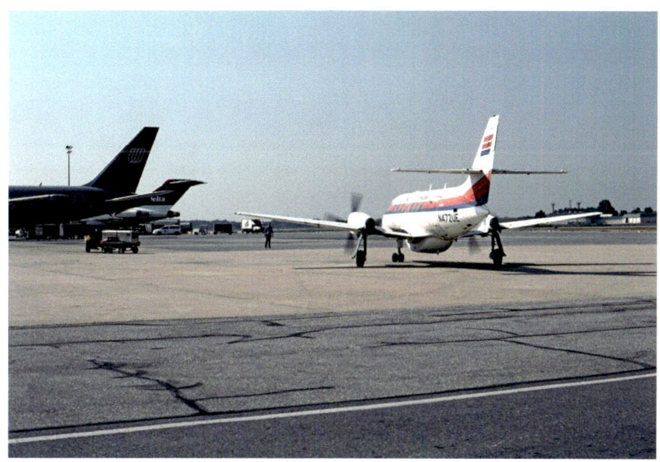

This is a relatively small regional turboprop aircraft, a BAe (British Aerospace) Jetstream 32, a nineteen-seater. It is being operated by Atlantic Coast Airliners for United Express and is about to depart.

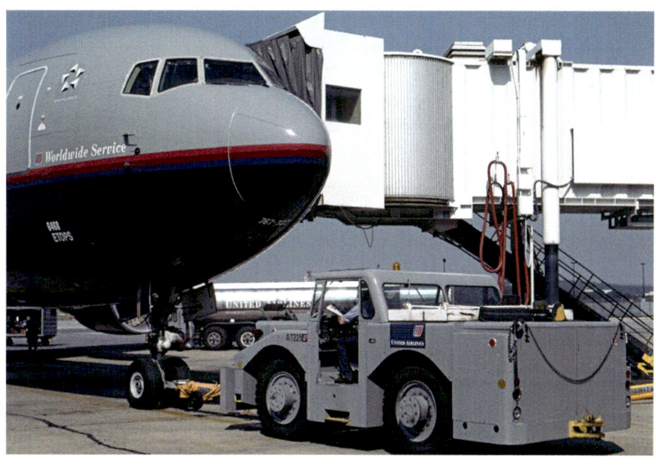

N668UA, a United Airlines Boeing 767-300, looks like it will be ready for pushback shortly, once those bags in the cart seen under the aircraft's belly are loaded.

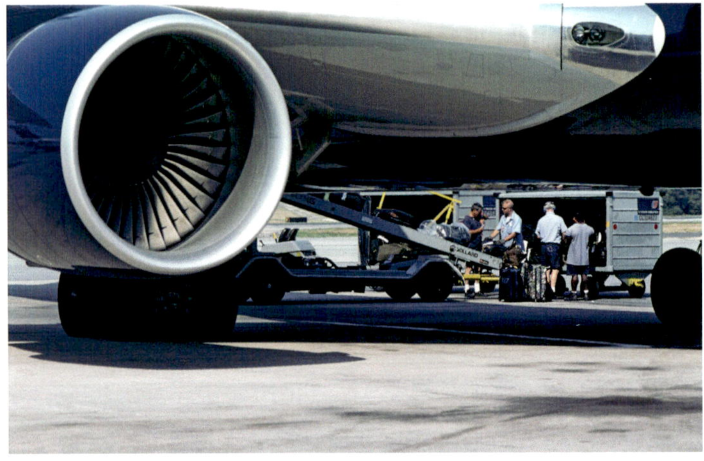

Here is a close look at one of N668UA's Pratt & Whitney turbofan engines, along with the ongoing bag loading.

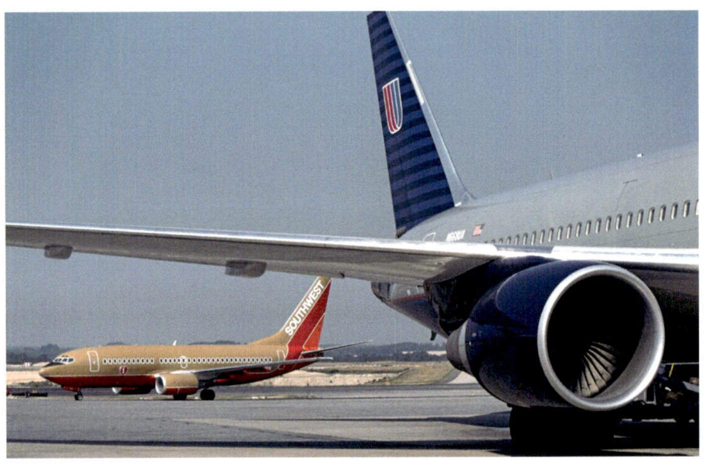

Looking to the left, a Southwest 737-700 taxies by the United 767.

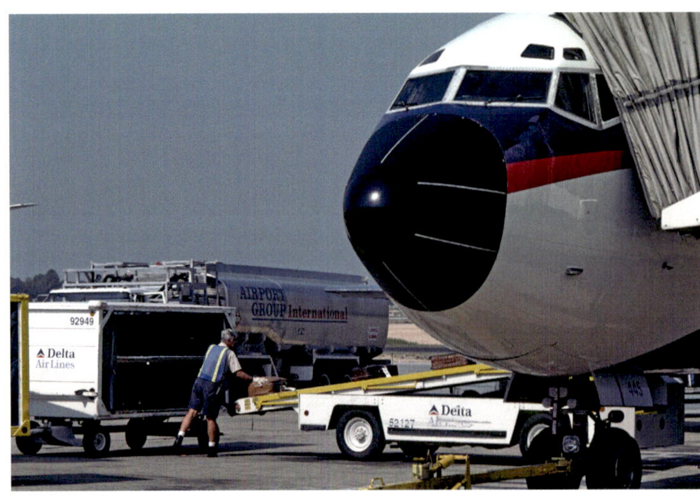

Unloading bags, this time from a Delta Airlines 727-200, N445DA.

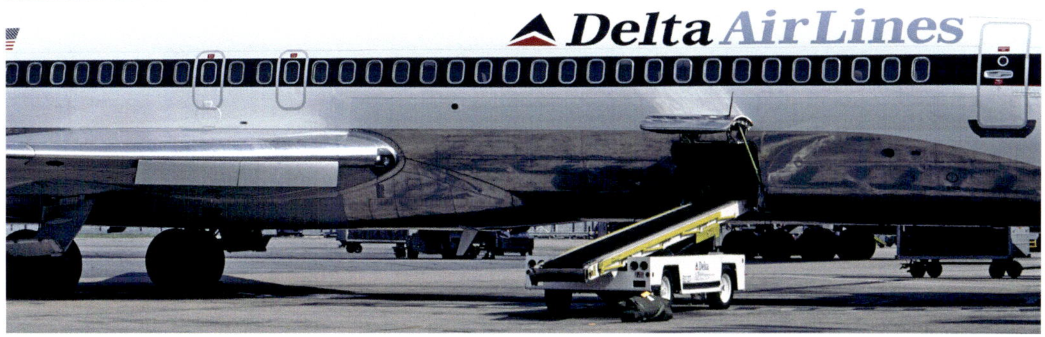

That task completed on N445DA, the belt loader rests, and the ramp is, briefly, unoccupied, although that is likely to change soon. Delta was a latecomer to using the 727, the most popular airliner in the 1970s, acquiring its first of the type only in 1972, following its acquisition of and merger with Northeast Airlines. DL would make up for lost time, however, eventually becoming the largest operator of the tri-jet type.

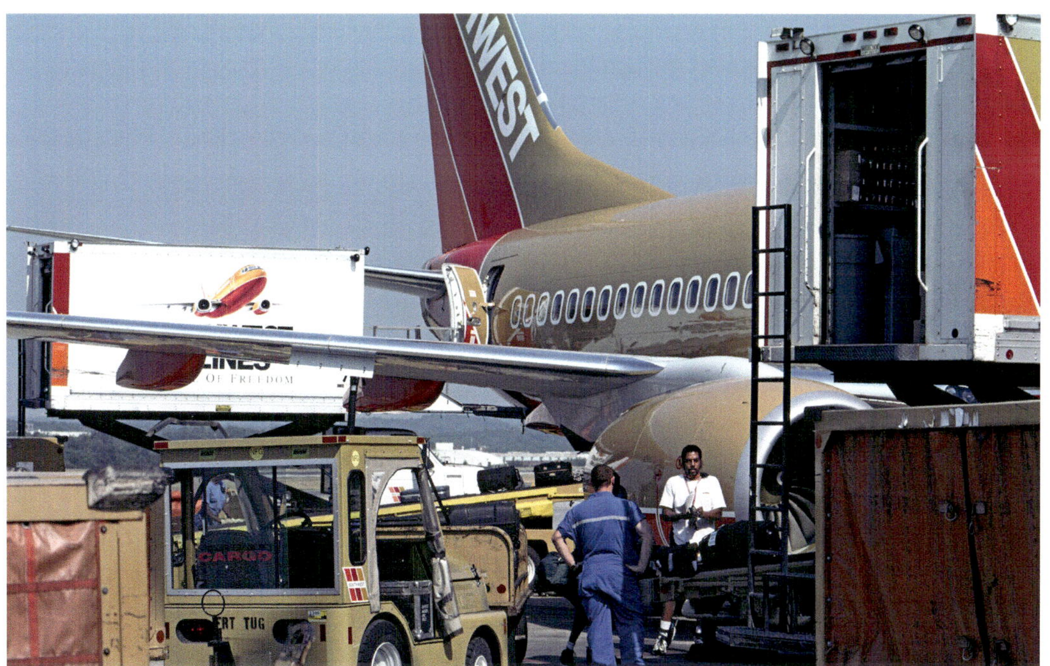

In contrast with the previous photo, ramp space is at a premium as this Southwest 737 is serviced at the gate!

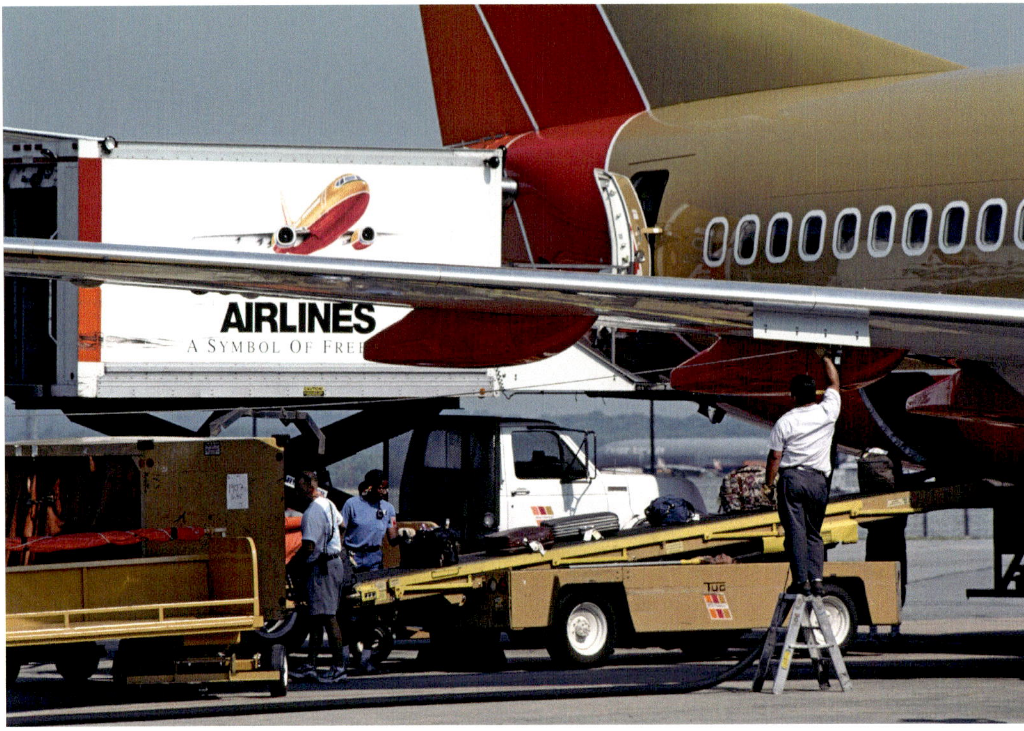

In addition to what was going on in the last picture, fueling is taking place on this 737, as well.

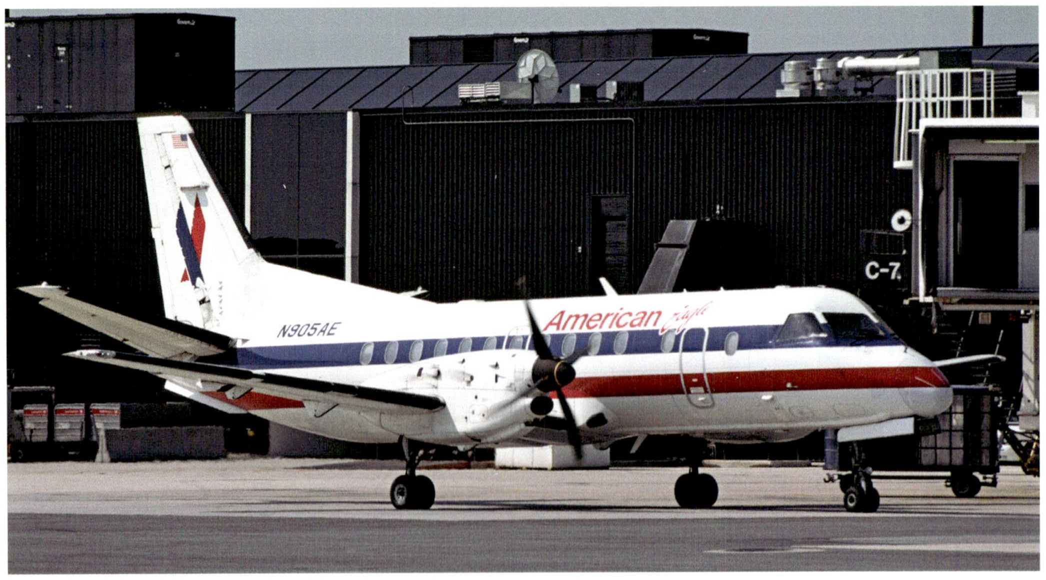

Here is another type of regional turboprop aircraft in the form of a Saab 340. N905AE is also operating for American Eagle, serving smaller, and often, shorter-distance markets than the EMB-145 that we saw earlier.

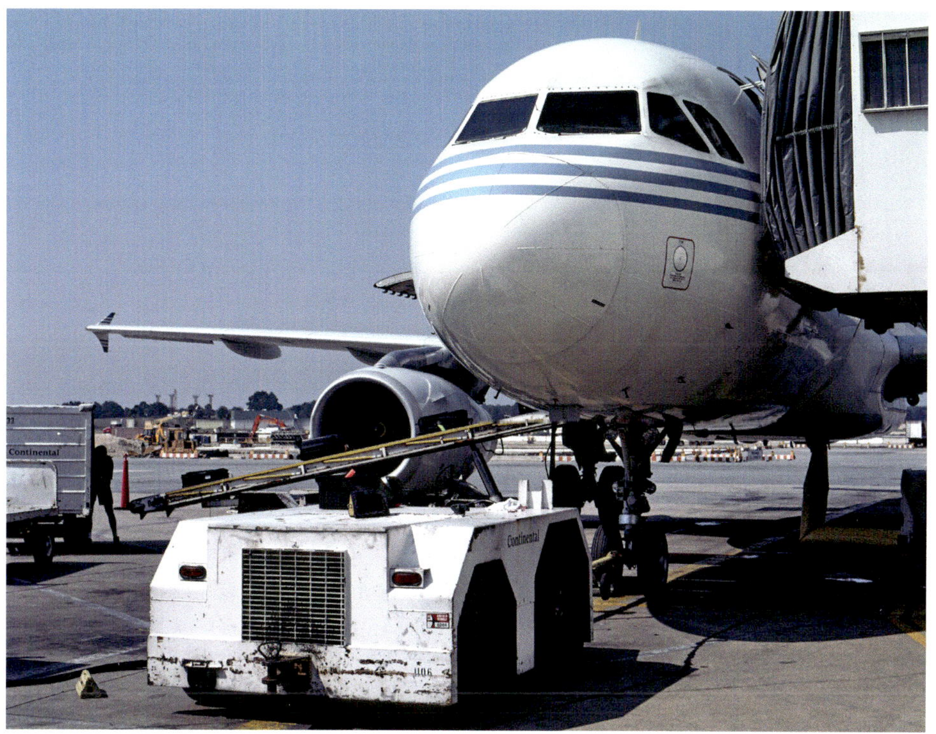

Now fueled, N622AW is getting closer to departure.

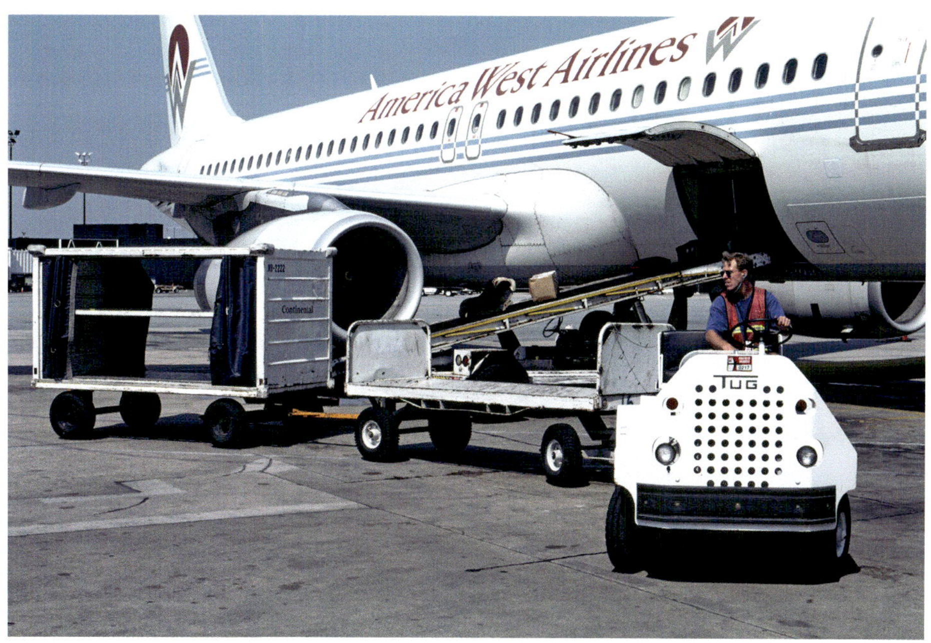

Just a few more bags for N622AW!

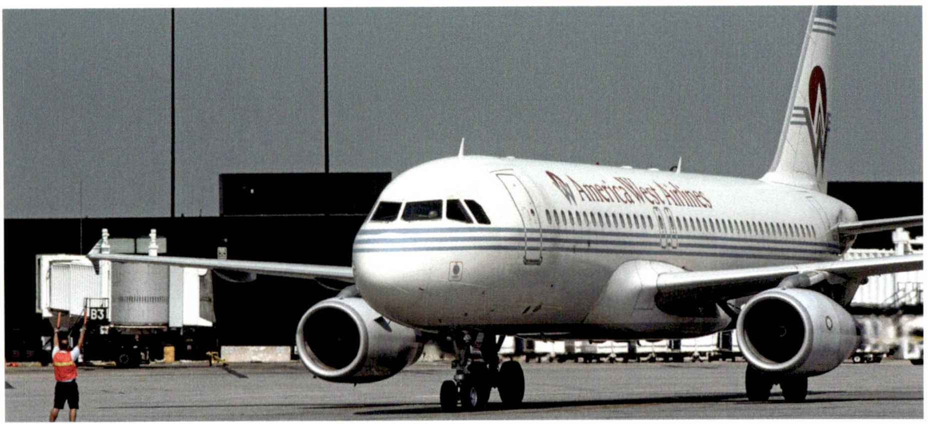

Soon the wands holding N622AW back will be lowered, and it will be on its way to the runway.

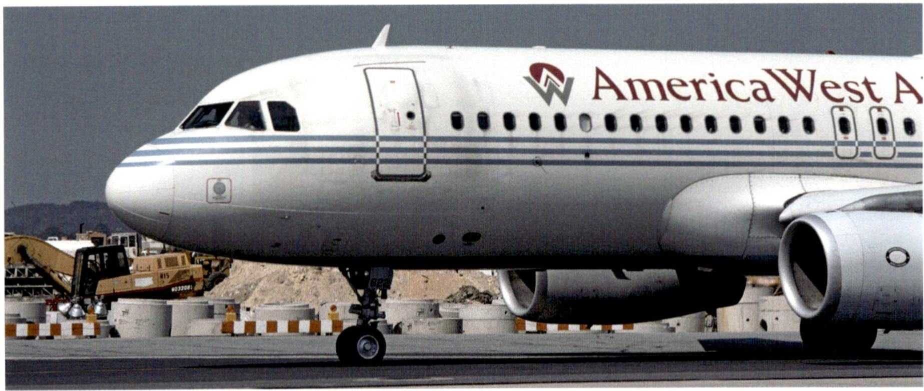

The ramp crew has done its job; N622AW's further progress will now be the rEsponsibility of ground control.

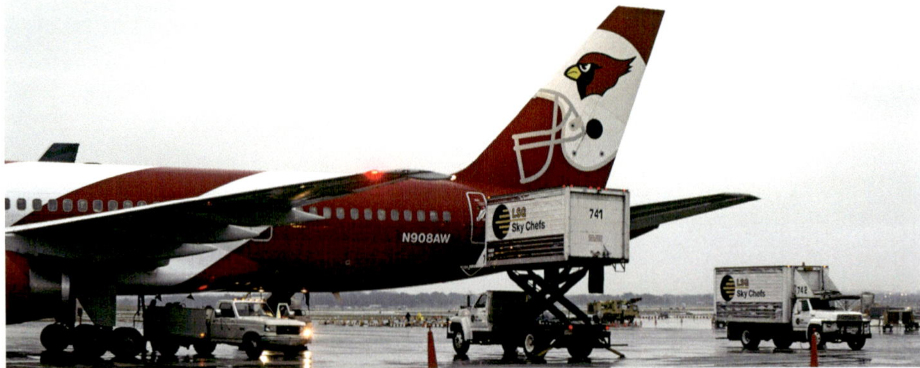

Not every day on the ramp is sunny and pleasant, as we can see in this scene of turnaround servicing on America West's 757 N908AW, in a livery promoting the Arizona Cardinals football team.

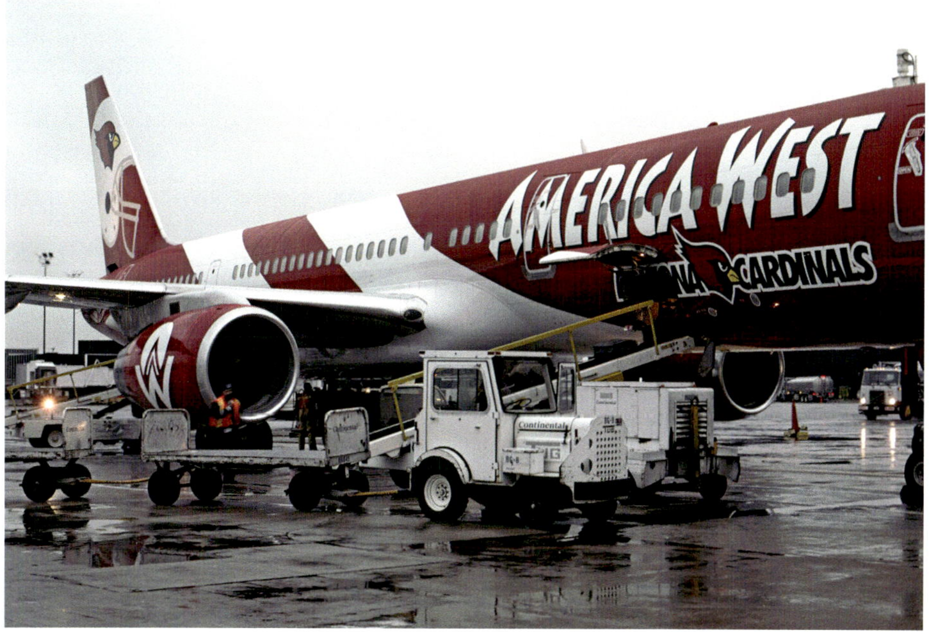

Baggage needs to be unloaded, weather notwithstanding, however. At least it is not actually raining right now.

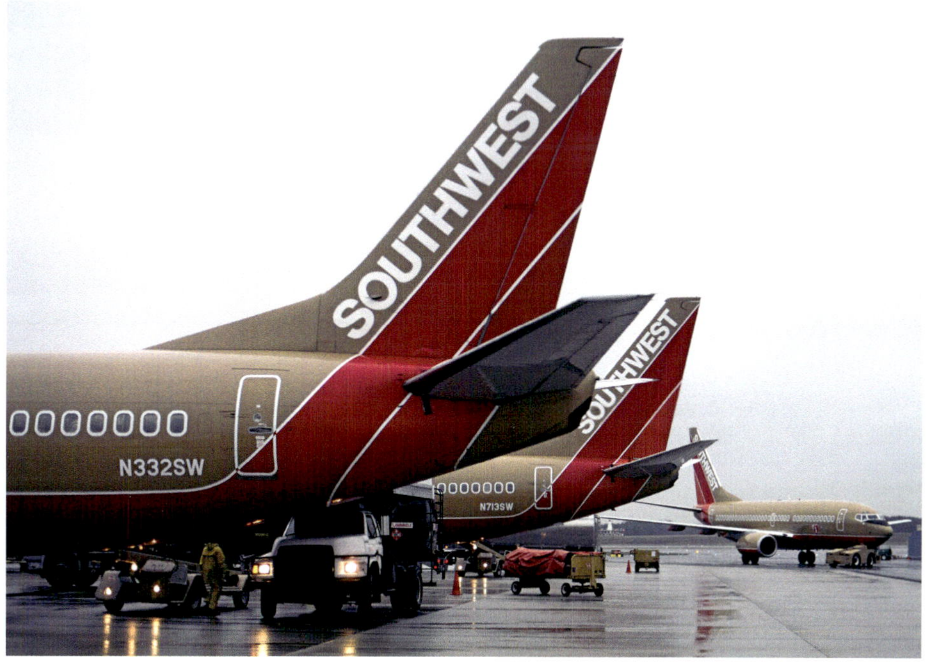

Three Southwest 737s (a pair of -700s, and a -300) are active on that airline's ramp. Two are parked at their gates, while the one on the right is being pushed back for departure.

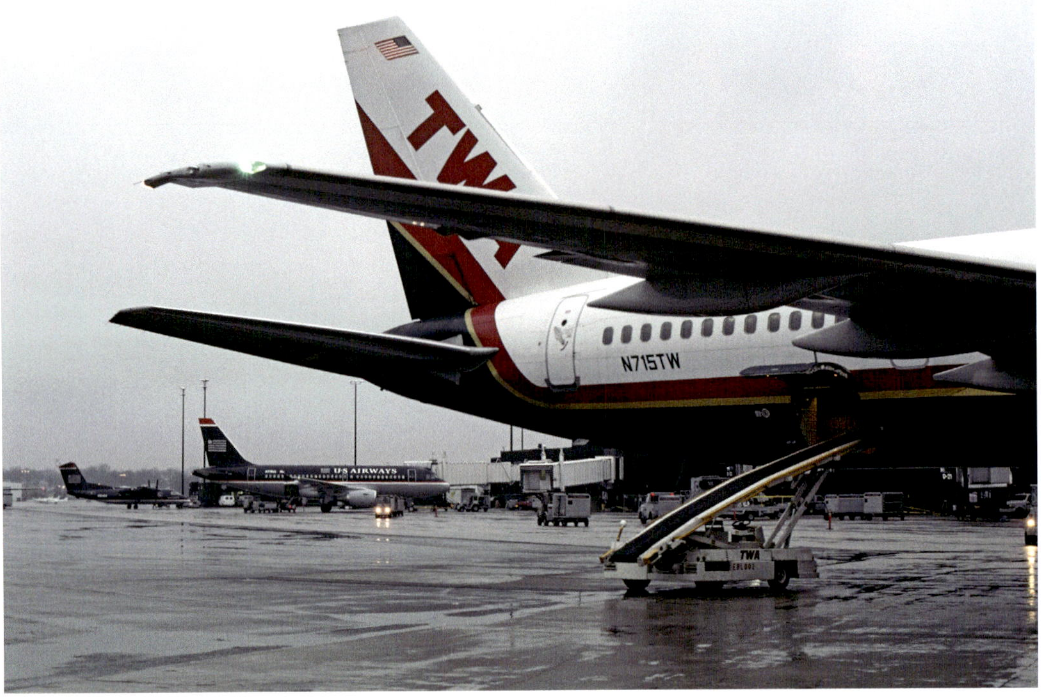

A TWA 757 is ready to receive customer baggage, while a US Airways A319 and a Dash 8 from that airline's commuter affiliate await further activity.

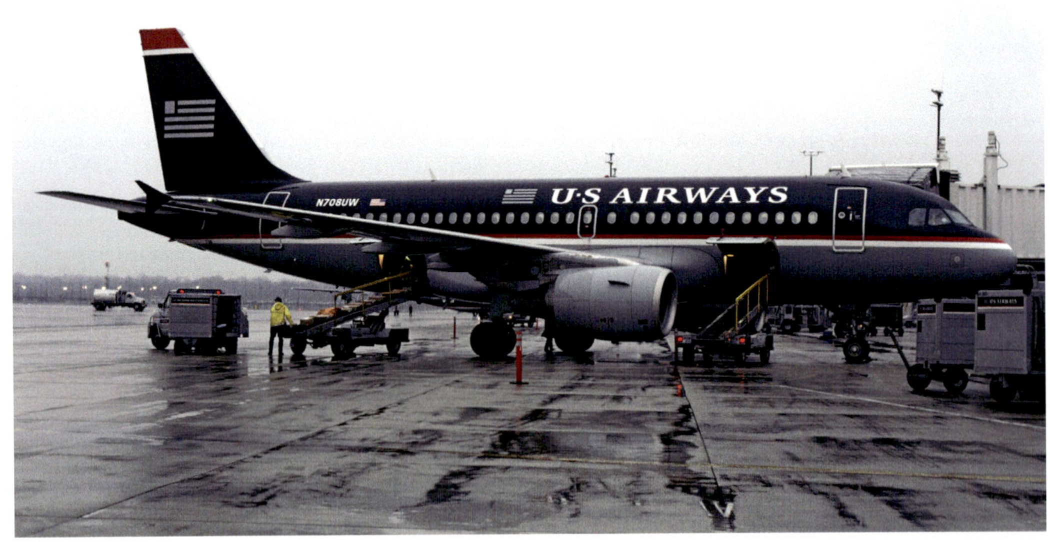

A steady stream of suitcases is going into the rear belly of N708UW, while all is calm, at least for the moment, at the front of the aircraft, on this side.

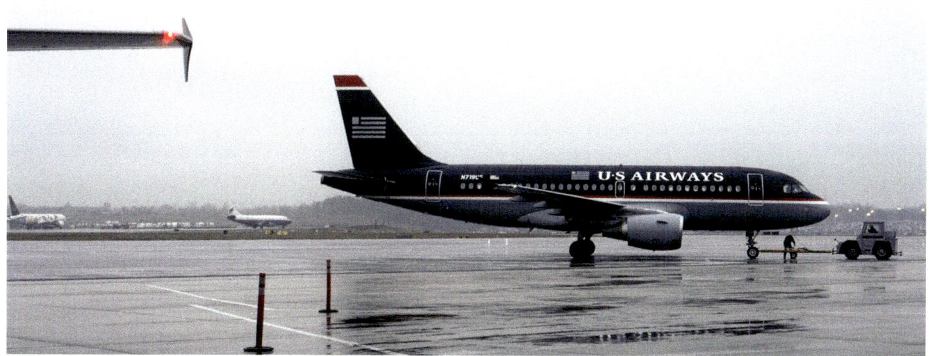

Nearby, another US A319, N719US, is in the process of having the towbar removed so that it can taxi away on its own.

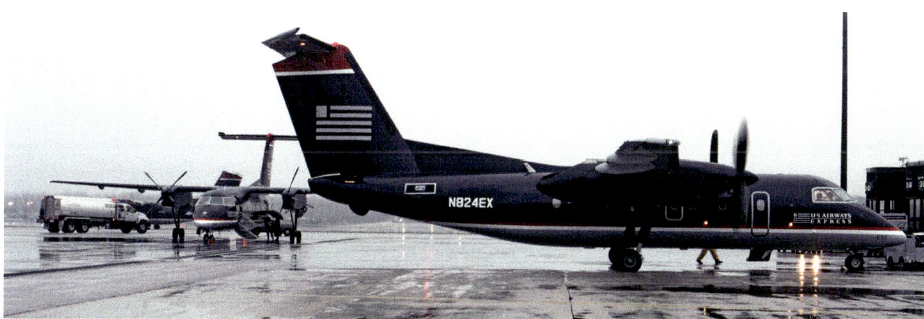

Nearby, a pair of US Airways Express Dash 8 turboprops can be seen; in the foreground, N824EX has the number two prop turning already, although the integral airstair on the other side of the aircraft has not been closed yet.

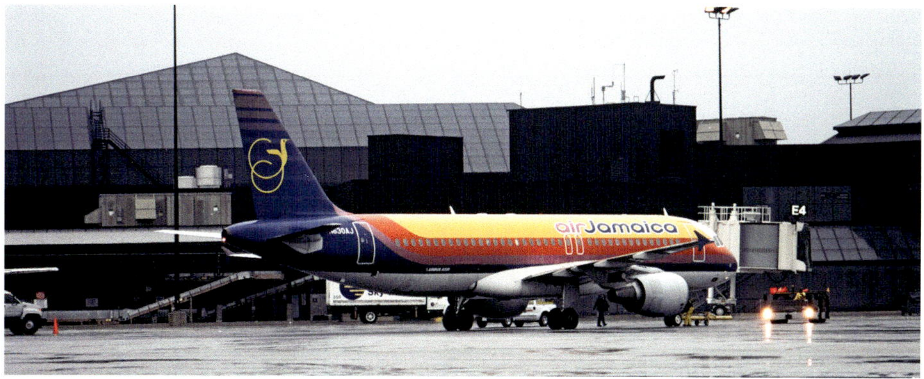

On Concourse E, Air Jamaica's A320 N630AJ is powered up, and almost ready to leave the gate area. The warm sun and pleasant temperatures likely at its destination probably will be very welcome to both the passengers and crew on board the aircraft.

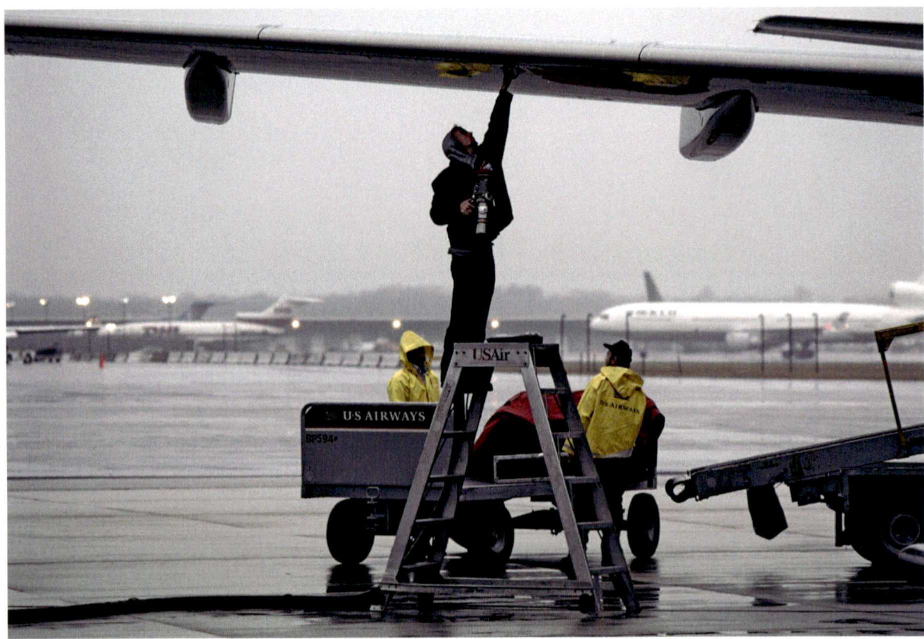

The need for fuel for the aircraft (in this case a US Airways A319) continues, inclement weather notwithstanding. At least the wing will provide some shelter for the ground crew while this is taking place. Over on the cargo ramp are freighters spending the day, or at least some portion of it, as well as a World Airways MD-11

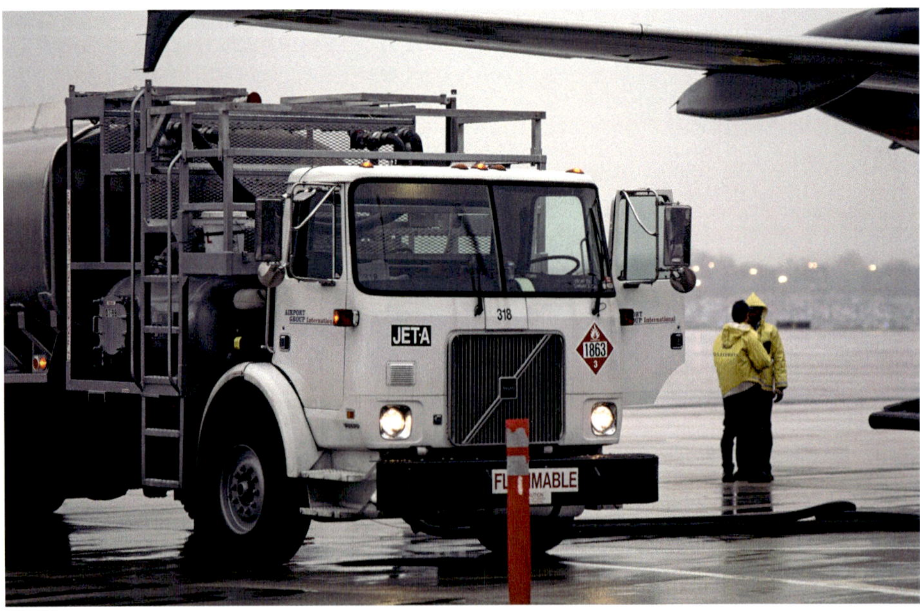

While the refueling is in process, two of the ground crew confer; given the not-so-pleasant nature of the day, the weather could well be the topic of conversation.

On a nice day, the walkaround inspection of an aircraft by a member of the cockpit crew can be enjoyable; today, it is probably viewed more as a chore, but it still needs to be done. This view serves to illustrate that a 757, although not a "widebody," is a fairly large aircraft; few if any crew members have to duck to walk under the fuselage. Do not try that with a 727 or 737!

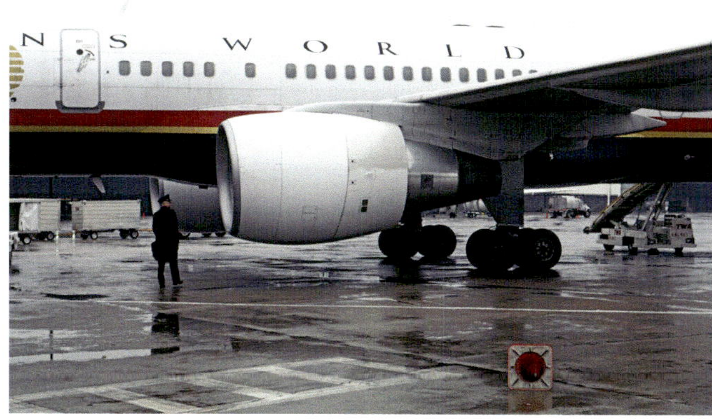

This "MetroJet" 737-200 depicts an attempt by mainline carriers (in this case, US Airways) to compete with LCCs (low-cost carriers) by having a so-called "Carrier Within a Carrier," with different, and usually more favorable (to the company), wages and work rules than the primary brand. It is now ready to push back. From a visual standpoint, it also illustrates the potential for reflected lighting produced by the wet ramp.

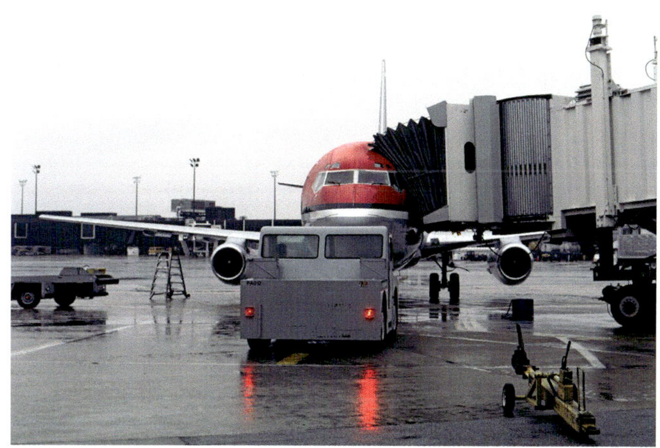

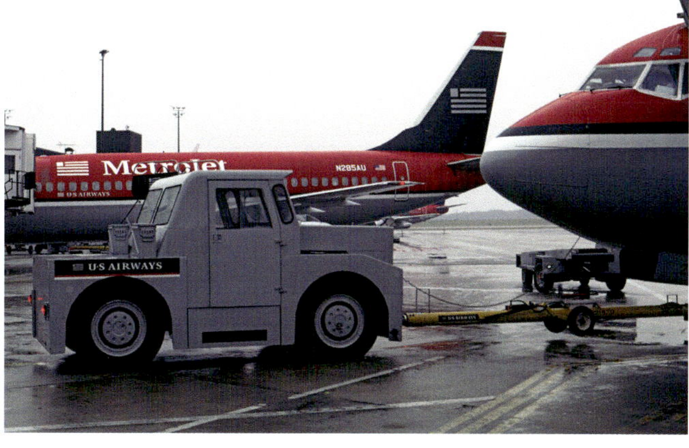

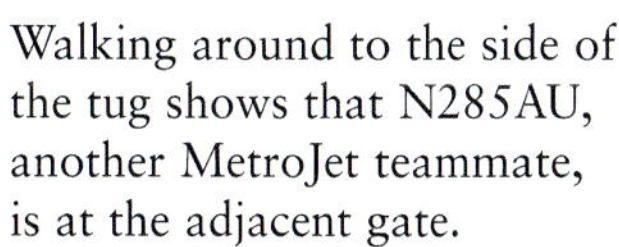

Walking around to the side of the tug shows that N285AU, another MetroJet teammate, is at the adjacent gate.

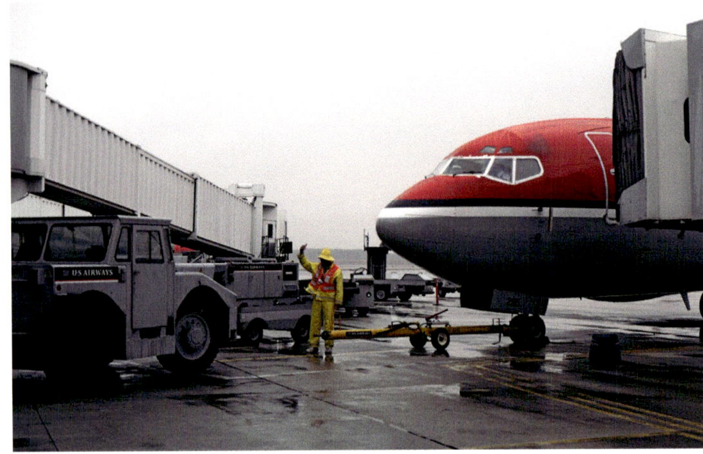

Shortly, the tug that will push N285AU is being guided towards the aircraft in preparation for attaching the towbar.

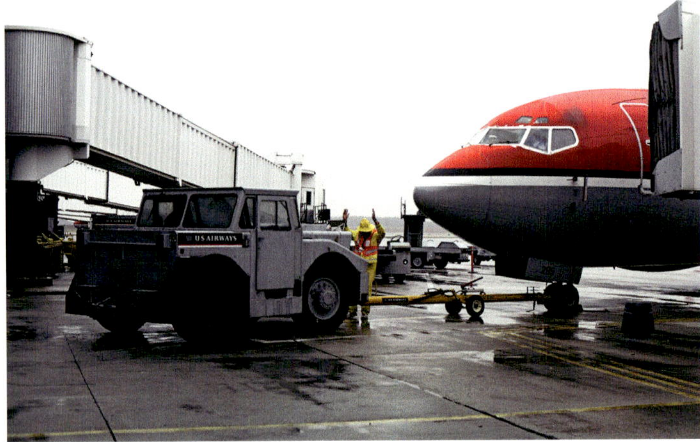

"Just this much to go."

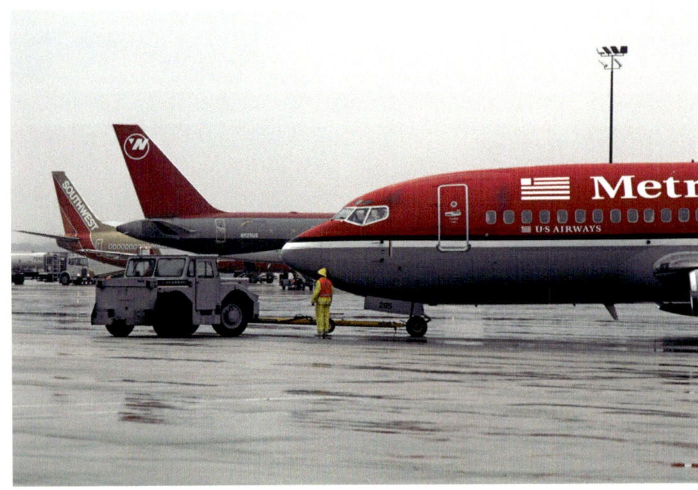

A short while later, and N285AU has been pushed back from the gate; over on Concourse C are a Southwest 737 and a Northwest 757.

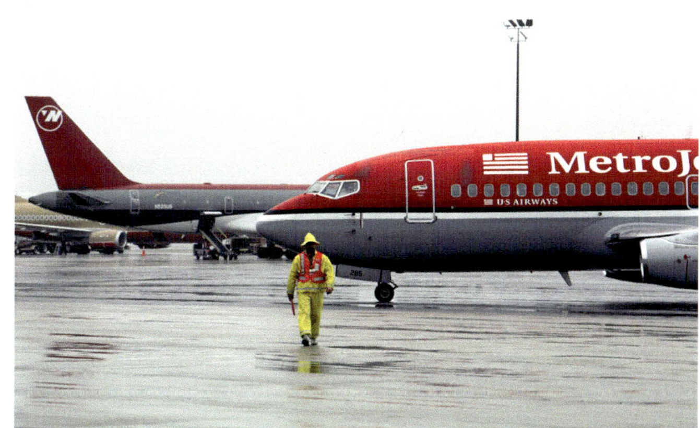

Pushback and tug exit complete, the worker directing the pushback leaves the ramp.

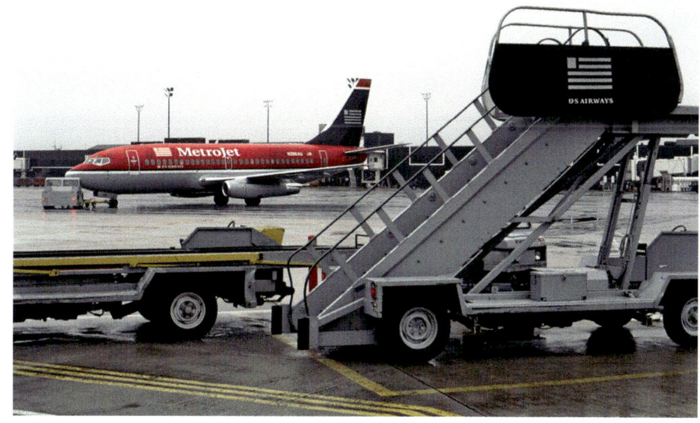

There is considerable MetroJet activity at the moment, as N288AU also is getting ready to head for the departure runway, with a belt loader and set of company airstairs looking on.

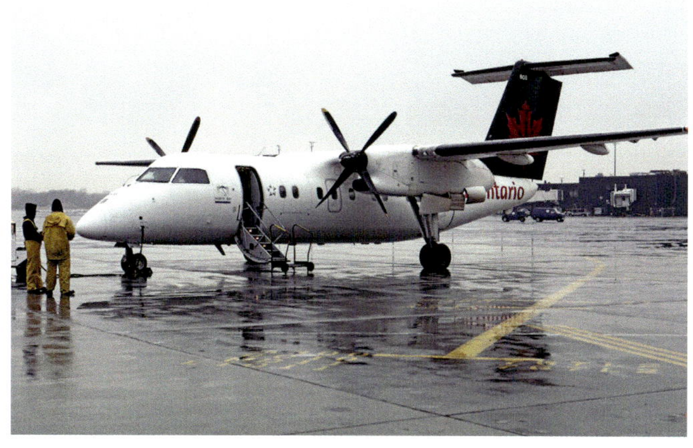

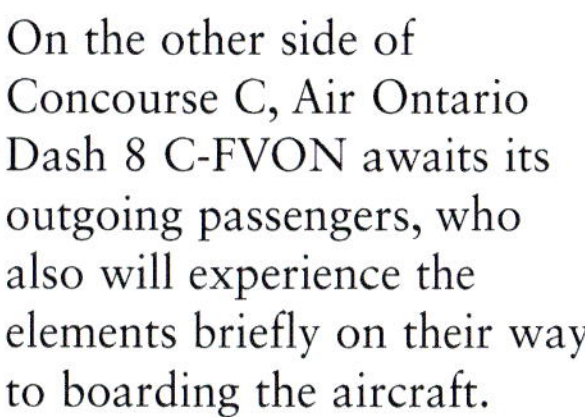

On the other side of Concourse C, Air Ontario Dash 8 C-FVON awaits its outgoing passengers, who also will experience the elements briefly on their way to boarding the aircraft.

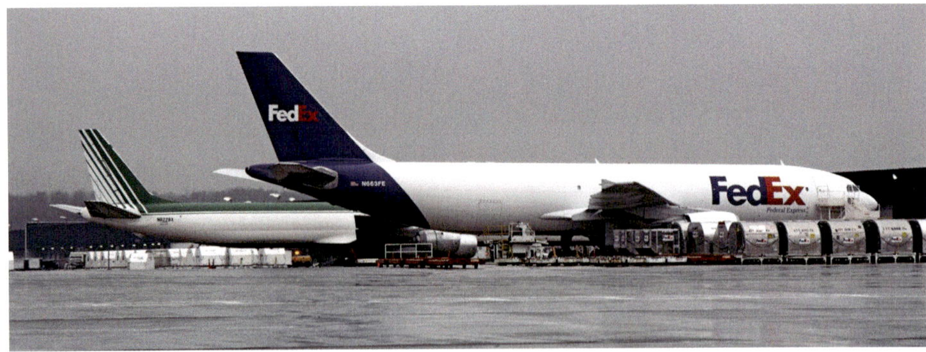

Visible on the cargo ramp are a FedEx A300-600 freighter and BAX Global's DC-8-71F N822BX, as well as lots of FedEx containers, for both the main deck, to the right, and lower deck containers for the belly, seen under the wing.

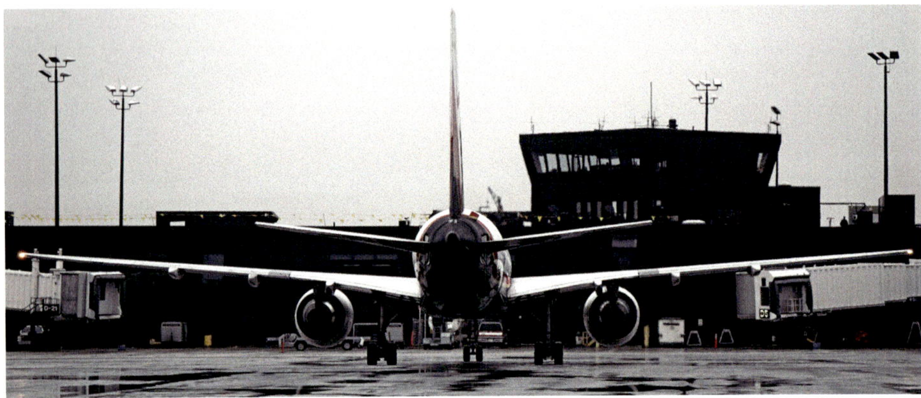

TWA's 757 N715TW has been pushed back from the gate, and the pushback vehicle has left the scene; time for engine starts.

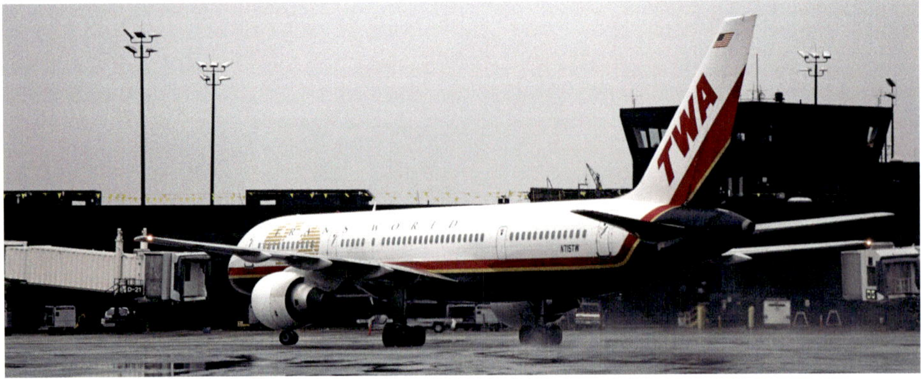

Now moving under its own power, this view of N715TW shows why even when it is not actively raining, you do not want to be in close proximity to the aircraft when it taxies on days like this one.

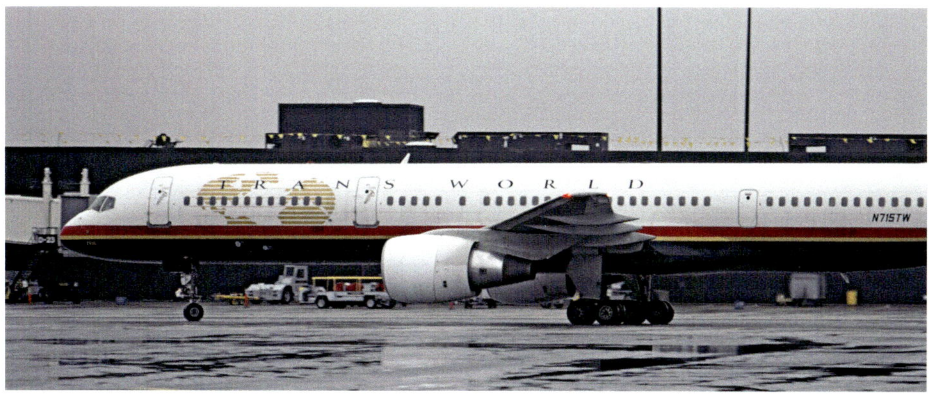

Standing safely off to the side, it is easy to see that this striking livery looks good even on a dull day, light-wise.

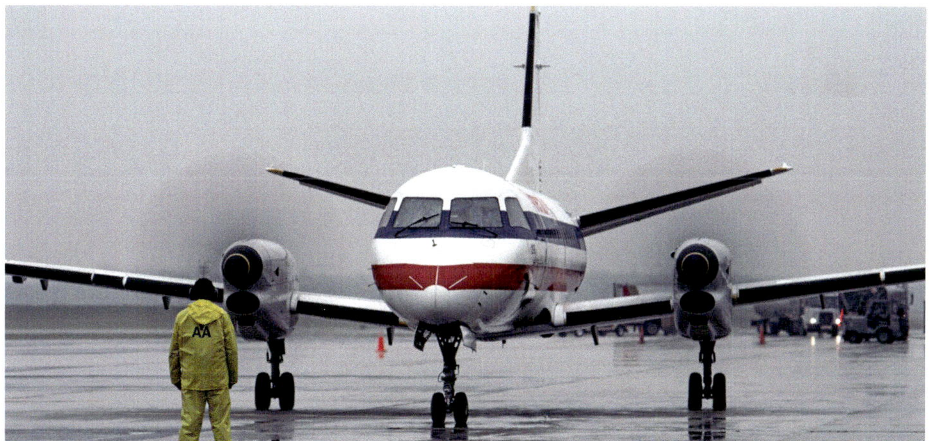

It should not be hard to discern that the passengers on this American Eagle Saab 340 are probably enjoying their immediate experience more than the ramp worker!

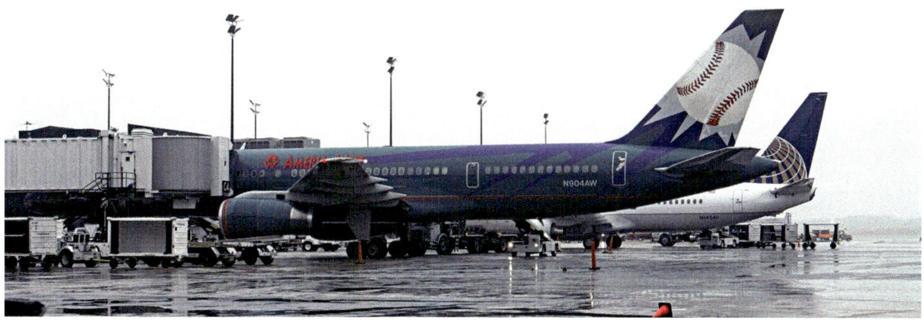

N904AW, an America West 757, is decorated to honor the national pastime, baseball, in this case in the form of the Arizona Diamondbacks. Behind it is a then-relatively new Continental 737-800.

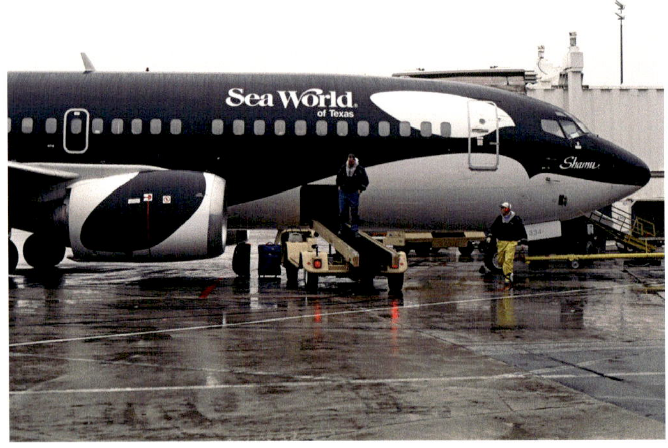

Southwest has had several aircraft named "Shamu" painted to represent killer whales in conjunction with promotions for Sea World of Texas. This is Shamu One, a 737-300; it looks like all the baggage off the inbound flight is on its way to the bag claim area.

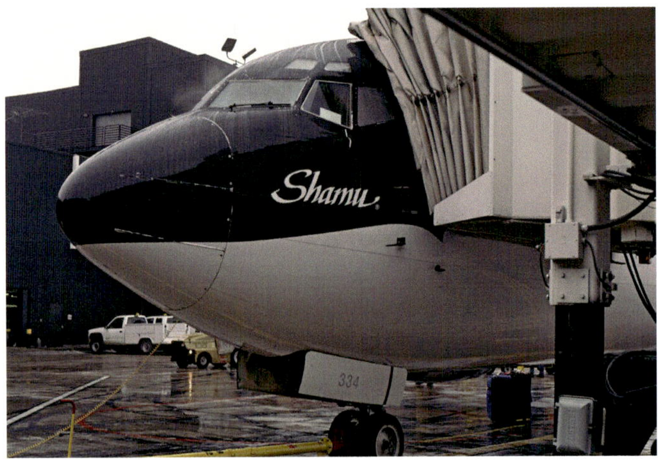

N334SW seems to be right in its element in the soggy ambient conditions.

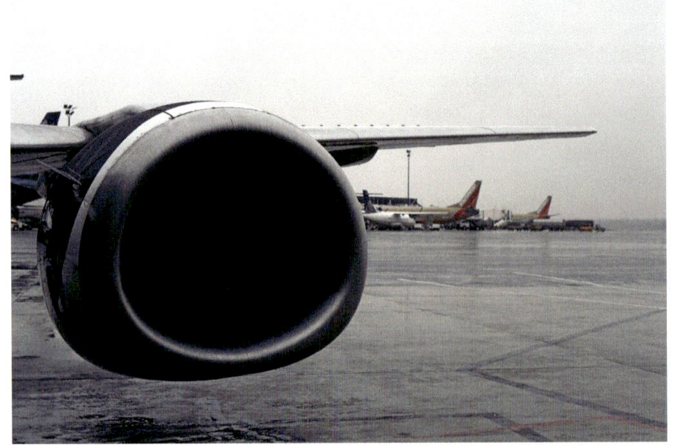

This view of the port wing and number two engine on N334SW illustrates how the nacelle enclosing the engines on this model of the 737 is actually oval-shaped, rather than round, in order to accommodate engine accessories while still maintaining adequate ground clearance.

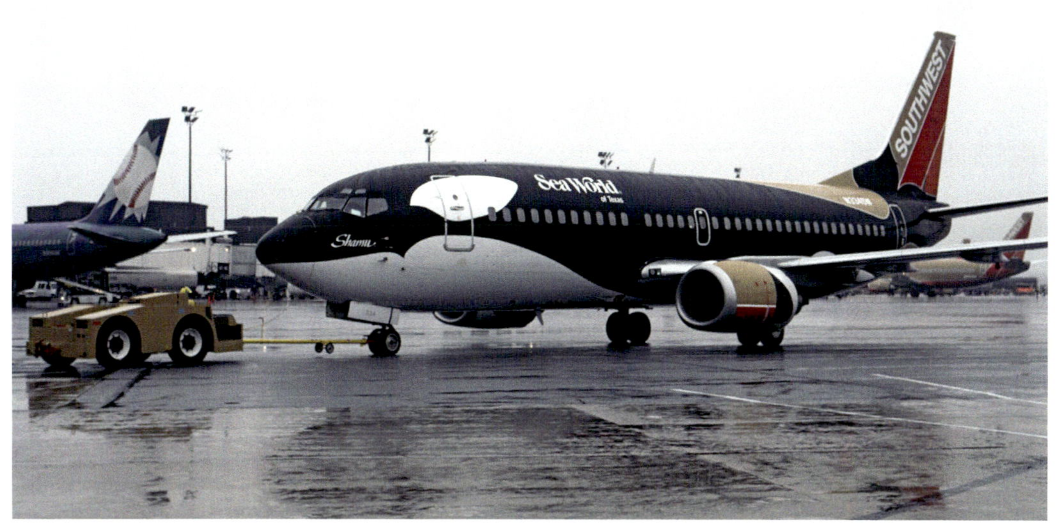

Refreshed and with a new load of passengers, it is time to go; shortly, this mechanical whale will again be swimming in the sky.

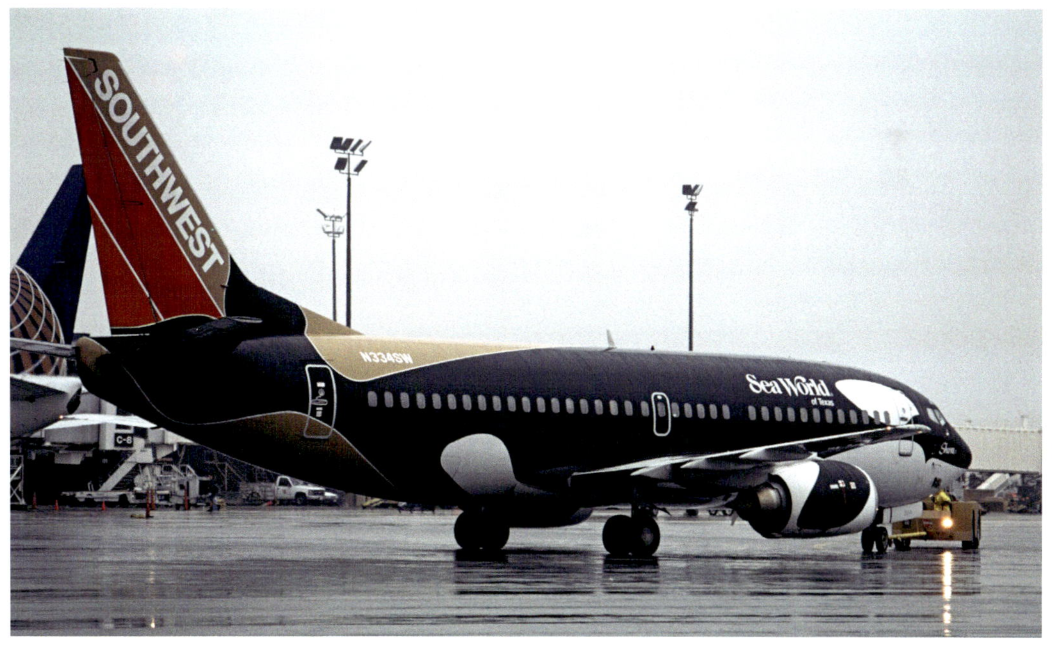

Shamu has left the gate and is about to return to the ocean of air that is its natural habitat. We will stay on the ground, of course, but next will be taking a look at "Prime Time" activity both on the ramp and out by the runways.

3

In Full Glory Reflected

As the daily routine progresses, activity begins to quicken when the morning shift personnel head for home in the afternoon. Short-haul movements continue as before, but long-haul arrivals, scheduled and charter, from both domestic and international locations, add to the mix of operations which have been occurring throughout the day.

During the afternoon/early evening peak, a full panoply of carriers is present. Some of them are making their once-a-day appearance, while the regulars who have been present throughout now bring out their chess pieces in full force. The flying colors of the aircraft liveries stand out in the late afternoon sun, almost like the racing silks of competing stables. This is an apt analogy, as what is occurring is a stakes competition, where winning is all-important, and there is little reward for placing, and virtually none for a third-place finish.

A fine place to observe the action is from the airport's fire and rescue station near the intersection of the landing and takeoff runways. Ascending and descending aircraft alternate, with a line of the former waiting on an adjacent taxiway, while a stream of aerial arrivals is visible in the sky beyond the touchdown point. What is on view is a veritable catalogue of commercial aircraft, with both domestic and international production represented. Included are both the pride of today's aerospace industry, as well as representatives of those which are now only historic names on the roster of aircraft manufacturers.

Arrivals can be dramatic, with variations in landing technique and ambient conditions causing some to settle gently onto the ground, while others produce more aural and visual evidence of their arrival, in the form of the squeals and smoke generated as the aircraft tires come back into contact with the ground. This also is an excellent location to observe different thrust reverser designs assisting in the transition from the aircraft's natural habitat—the sky—to ours.

Simultaneously, others are ascending skyward, some vaulting into the air almost immediately, while the longer-haul trips, especially those on international journeys, utilize the runway length more fully. As the sun gets closer to the horizon, the light takes on the quality photographers call "sweet," which results in increasingly bold limning of the bright, reflective surfaces of the aircraft against the more subdued elements of the surrounding airport infrastructure.

Over on the cargo ramp, the freighters are beginning to come to life, as fuel trucks pump their contents into the waiting aircraft, while the airplanes await the transfer of cargo into the yawning maws of their main-deck compartments. About the same time, the sunbirds which departed south in the morning begin to return, as well.

Needless to say, things are hectic on the ramp. Except for the trips returning from tropical destinations, virtually all the flight equipment present now needs servicing from both an inbound and outbound perspective. This is the main event; enjoy the front-row view of the action!

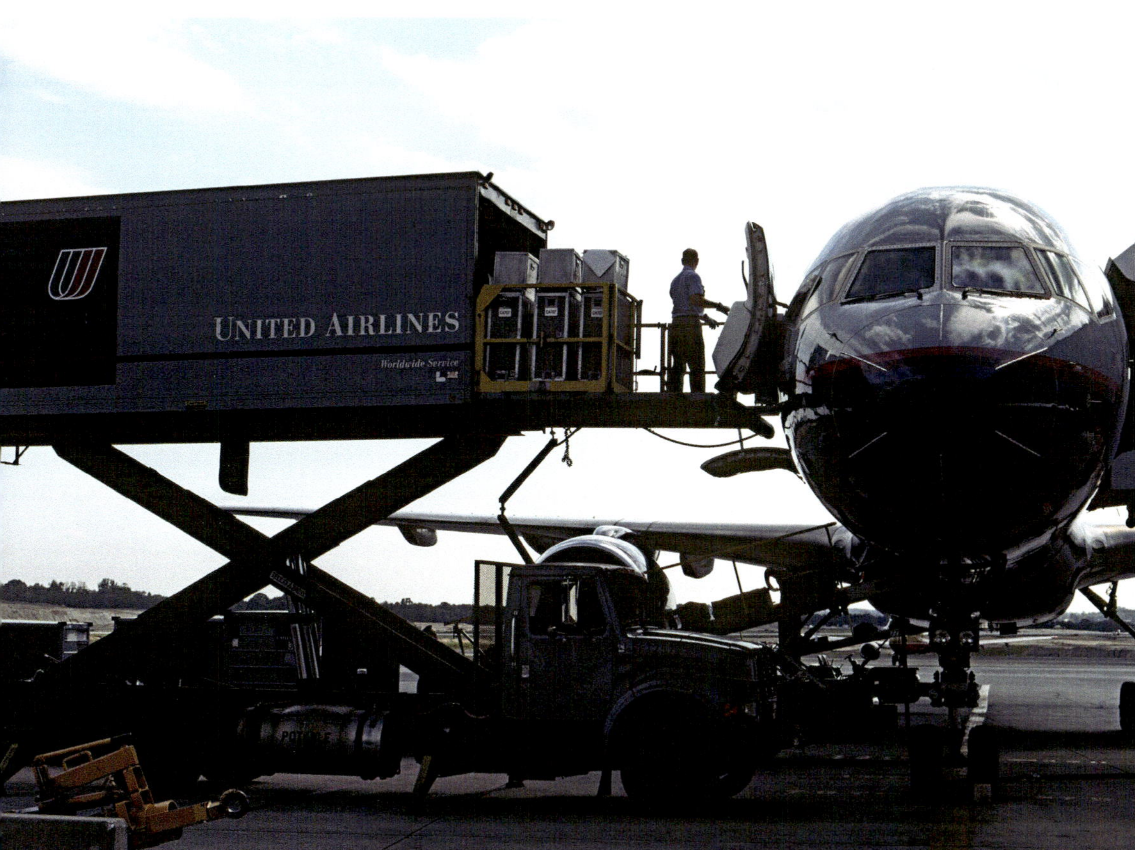

A United 757 has its forward galley serviced during its BWI turnaround.

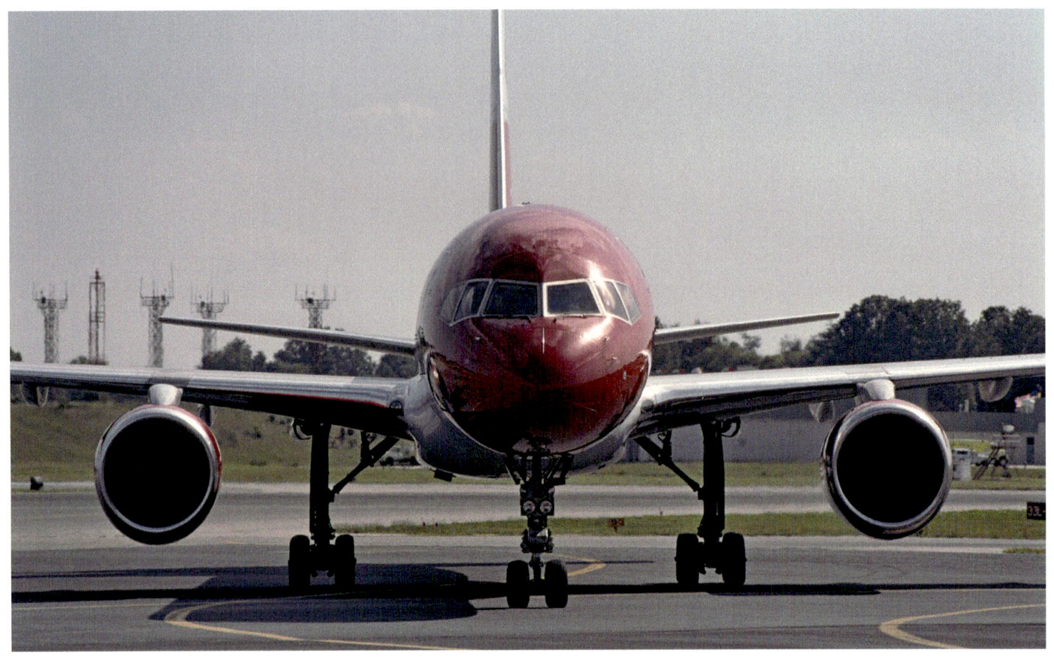

N908AW, which we have already seen earlier, arrives at BWI in the late afternoon.

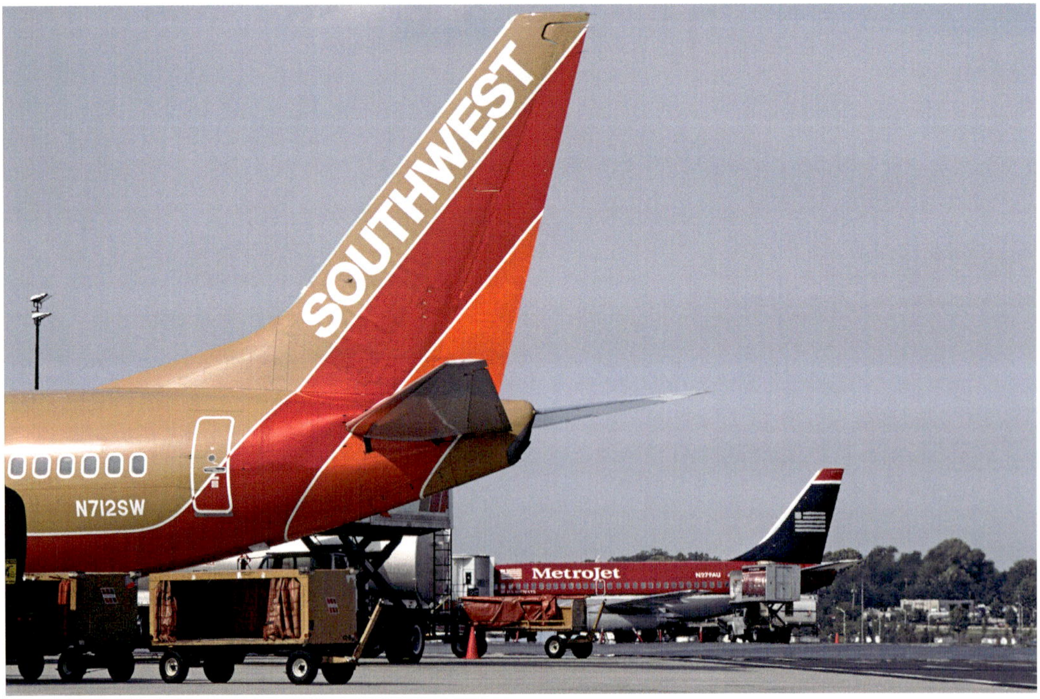

LCCs, in the form of Southwest 737-700 N712SW and MetroJet 737-200 N279AU, are at their respective gates.

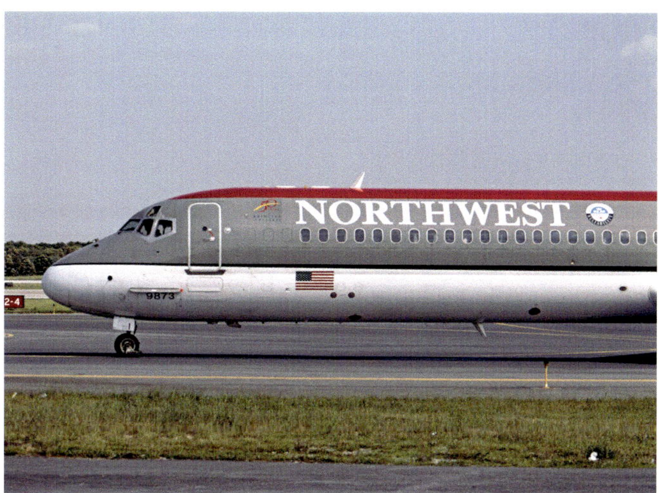

Northwest DC-9-50 N782NC passing by our vantage point. This aircraft was delivered to North Central Airlines and came into the Northwest fleet via that carrier's acquisition of Republic Airlines, which had resulted from the merger of North Central and Southern Airways.

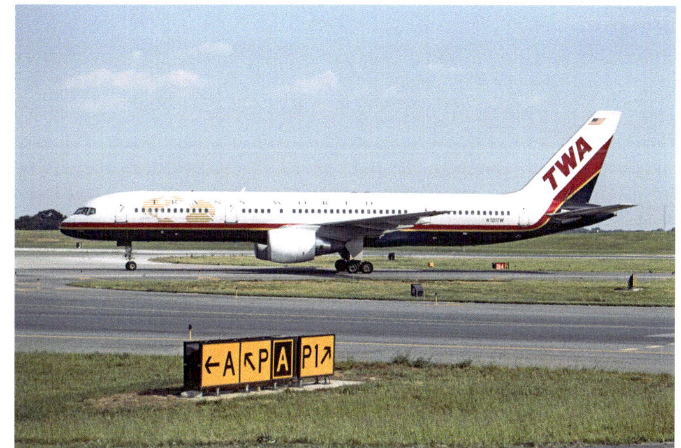

This turned out to be a good spot to stay awhile; next up was TWA 757 N701TW.

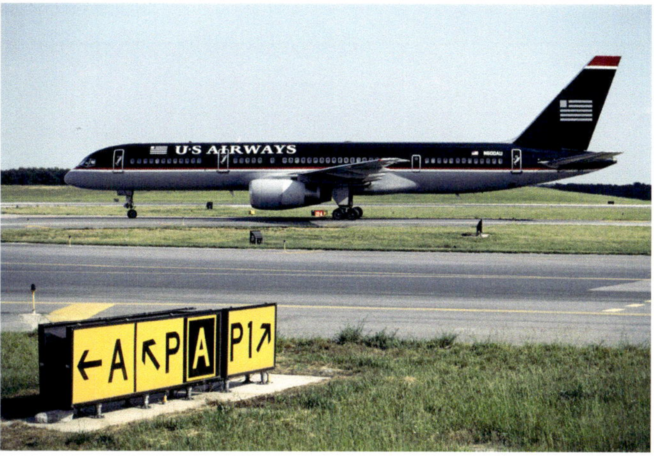

Another 757, N600AU of US Airways, followed the TWA aircraft. This relatively dark livery, with its stylized U.S. flag, was referred to as the "Darth Vader" paint scheme, reflecting the appearance of the villain of the *Star Wars* series of movies.

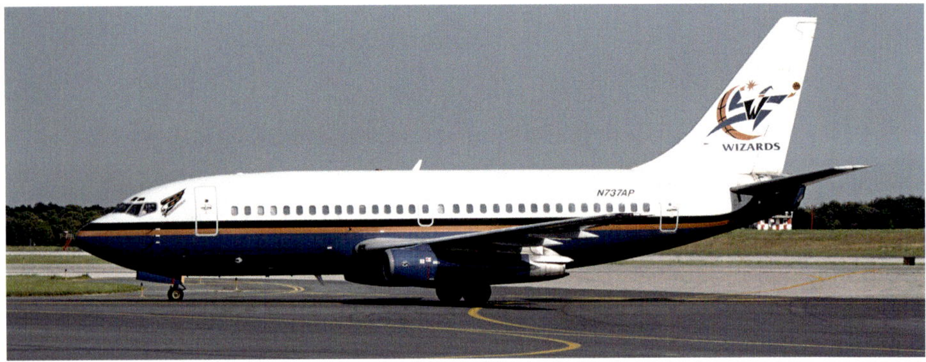

This 737-200, originally flown by United Airlines as N9075U, is now being operated by Pace Airlines for the Washington Wizards basketball team, which should not be a surprise, based on its paint scheme. The letter suffix in the aircraft's registration reflects the initials of the owner of the Wizards, Abe Pollin. The basketball Wizards had previously been the Baltimore, and later, the Washington Bullets.

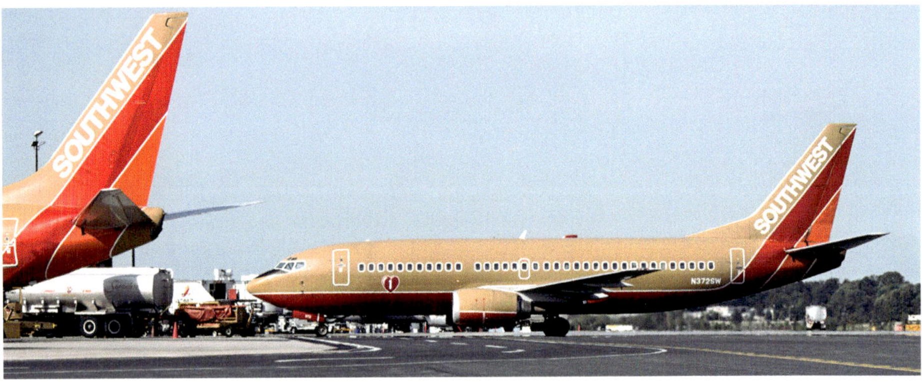

Close by, the Southwest ramp is busy during the late afternoon/early evening peak. Here, 737-300 N372SW is getting ready to taxi.

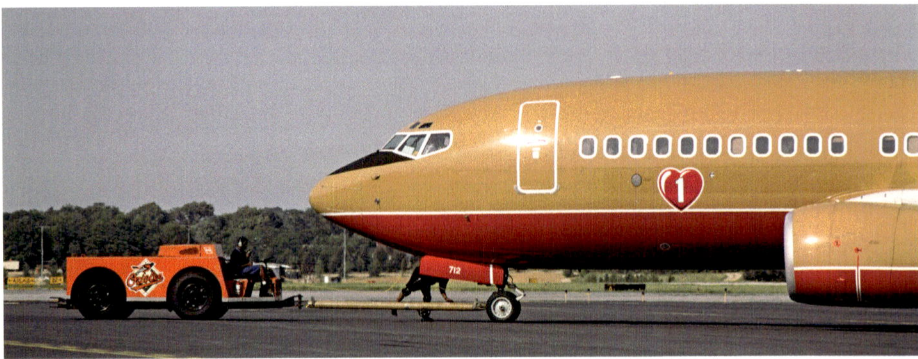

N712SW, a Southwest 737-700, has been pushed back by a tug bearing the logo and colors of the local baseball team, the Baltimore Orioles.

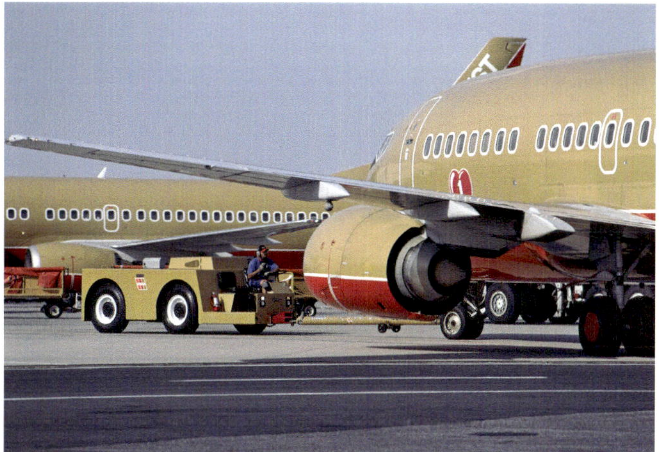

A 737-500, N512SW is being pushed back by a vehicle in Southwest's company colors, although it should be noted that its driver is wearing an Orioles baseball cap.

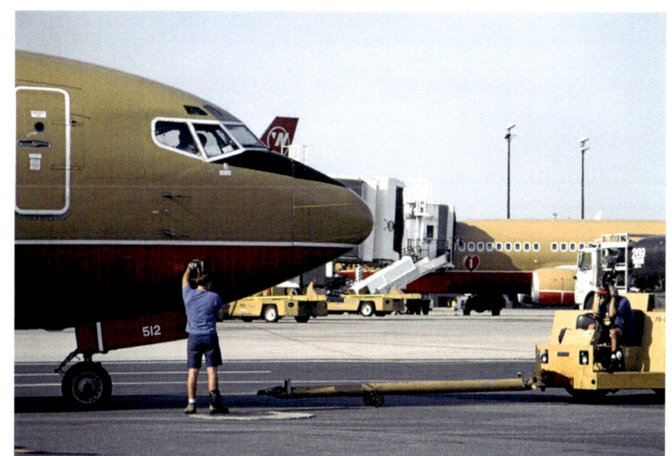

The tow bar has been disconnected from N512SW, and the ramper is letting the flight deck crew know that this has been completed.

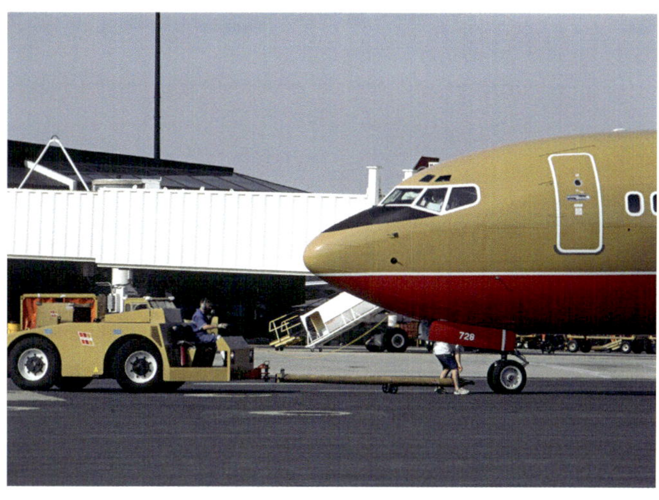

Southwest 737-700 N729SW also is now detached from the towbar and will shortly follow N512SW for departure.

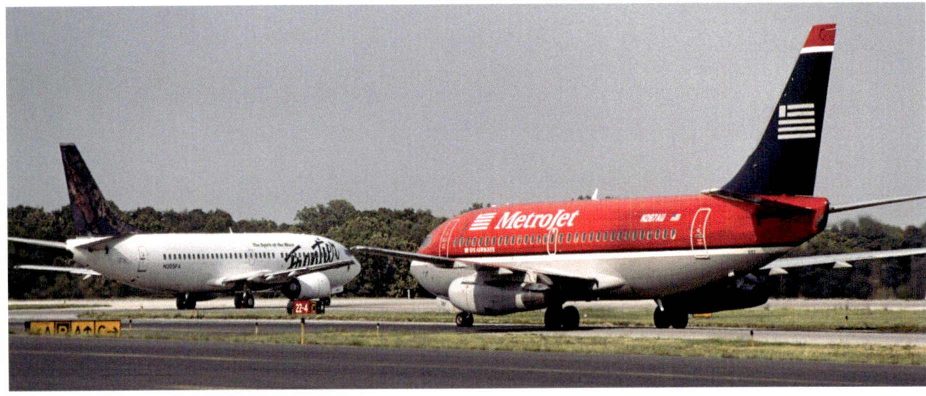

LCCs Frontier (N305FA, a 737-300) and MetroJet (N287AU) appear to be jockeying for position, although, in reality, the FAA traffic personnel in the BWI tower are firmly in charge of aircraft movements.

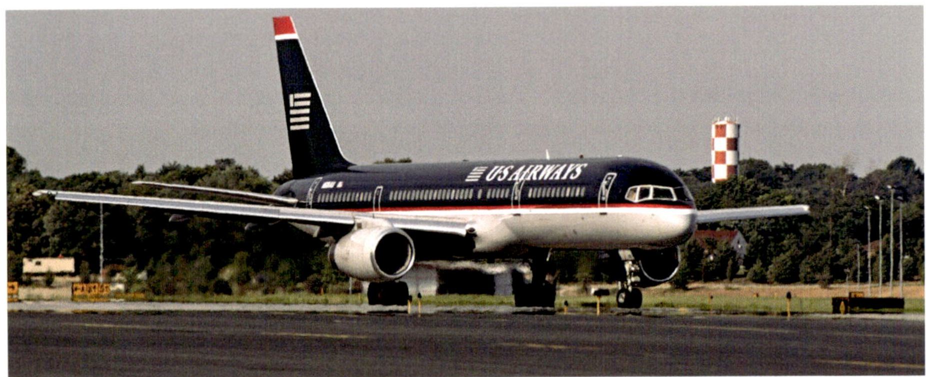

Another US Airways 757, N607AU, is seen taxiing here.

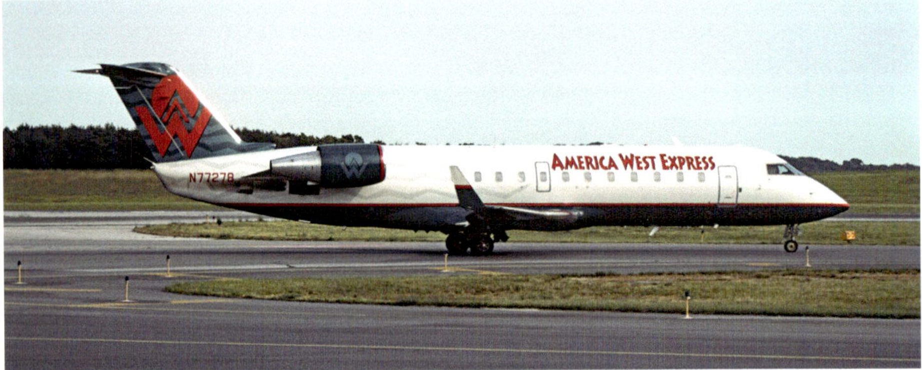

The regional jet "revolution," in terms of replacing slower, shorter-range turboprop aircraft, is picking up speed as of the late 1990s, represented here by Bombardier/Canadair's CRJ-200 N77278, being flown by Mesa Airlines for America West.

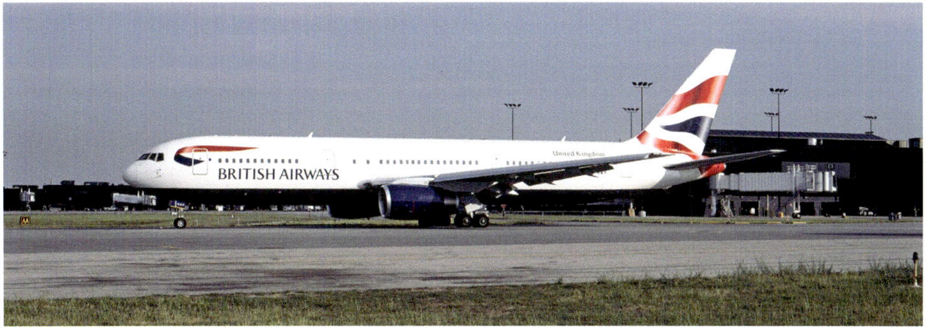

British Airways 767-300 G-BNWR has left the international terminal, and is taxiing to its departure runway, on the way to London, England's Heathrow International Airport.

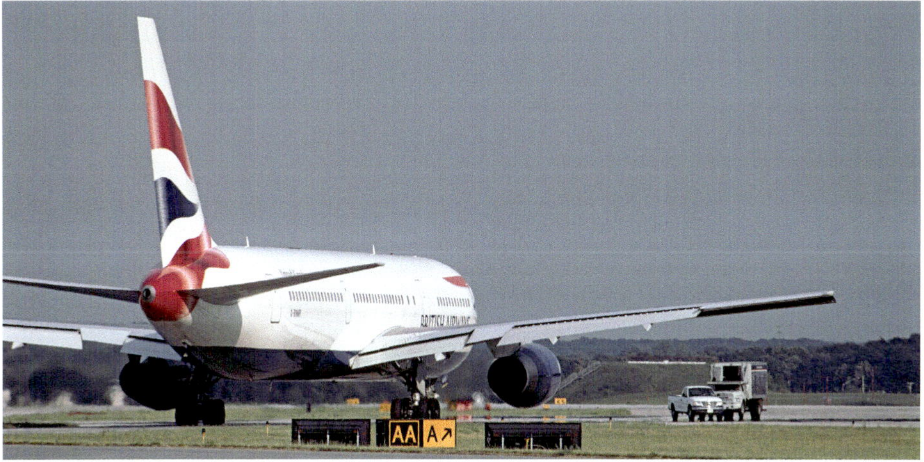

"Whiskey Romeo" has now turned the corner away from Concourse E and is heading for runway 28.

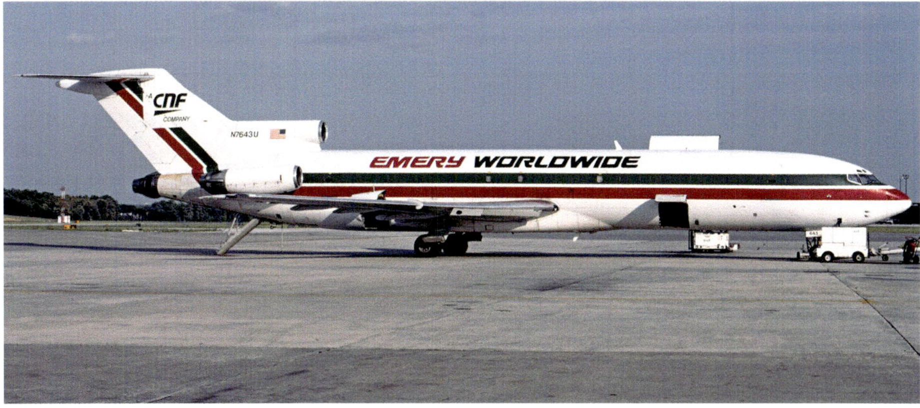

Over on the cargo ramp, Emery Worldwide's 727-200 freighter N7643U, another United Airlines alum, awaits upcoming activity a little later in the evening.

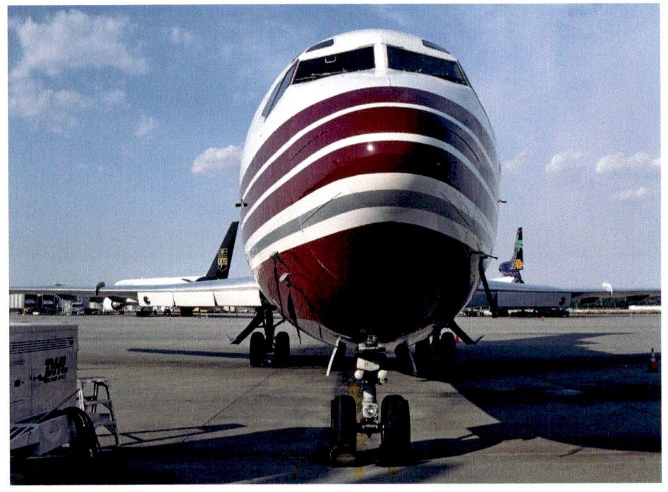

DHL's cargo 727-100 N706DH, also originally at United, gives the appearance of striking an "in your face" pose as it too waits for more activity once the sun has set.

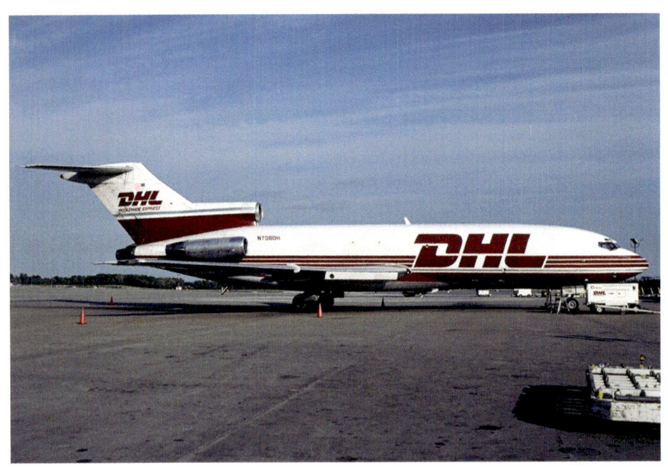

A more typical side portrait view of N706DH skips the drama of the previous shot.

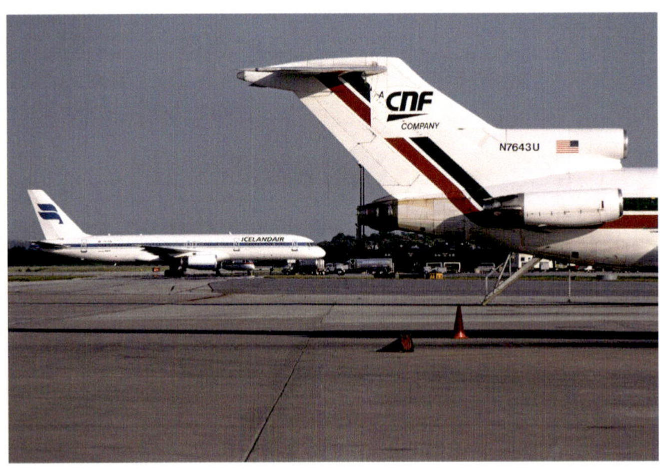

Icelandair's 757 TF-FIN arrives from its home country, and taxies by Emery's 727 on the way to the international terminal.

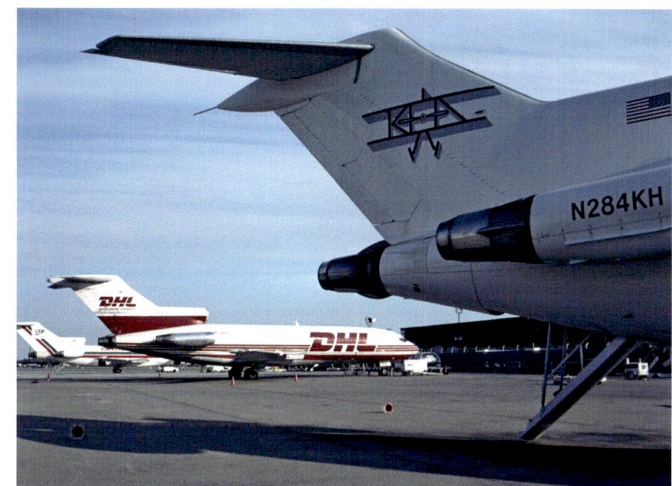

Kitty Hawk Air Cargo's 727-200 N284KH, previously at Air Jamaica, is also present near the Emery and DHL aircraft.

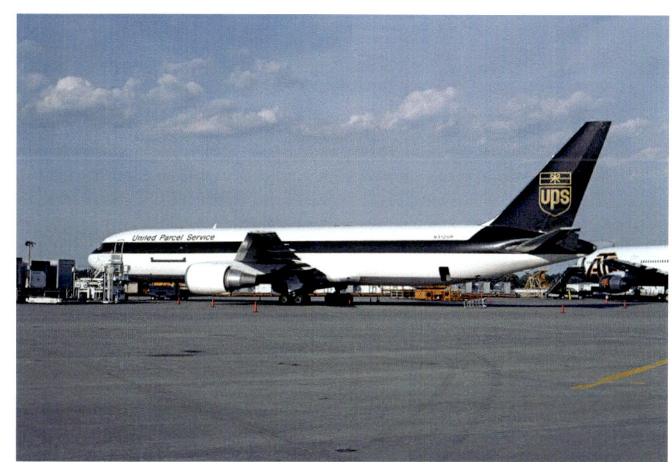

As yet, UPS' 767-300 N312UP lacks any visible activity, but that will change soon, as we will see.

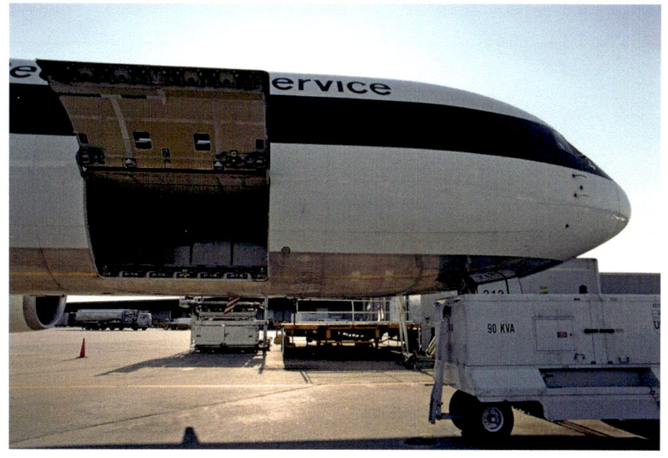

On display on the other side of N312UP is its capacious forward belly, as well as the cargo door capable of accommodating large containers and cargo pallets.

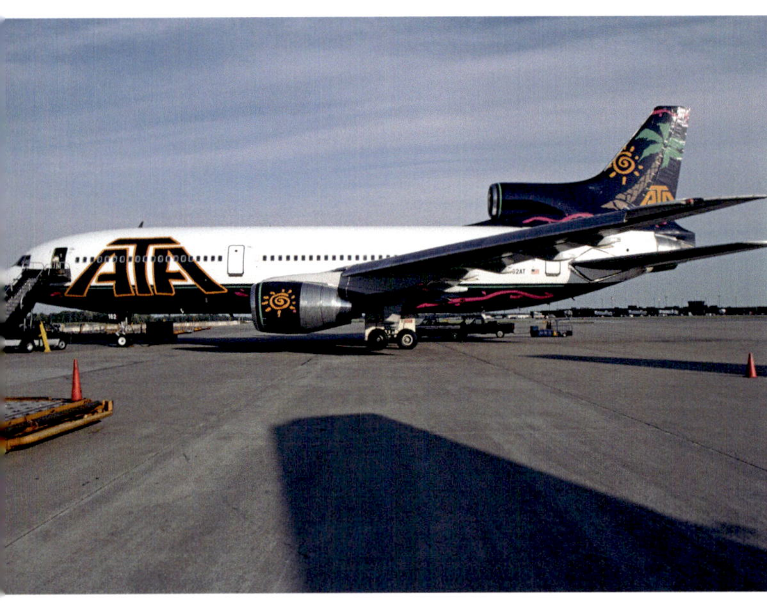

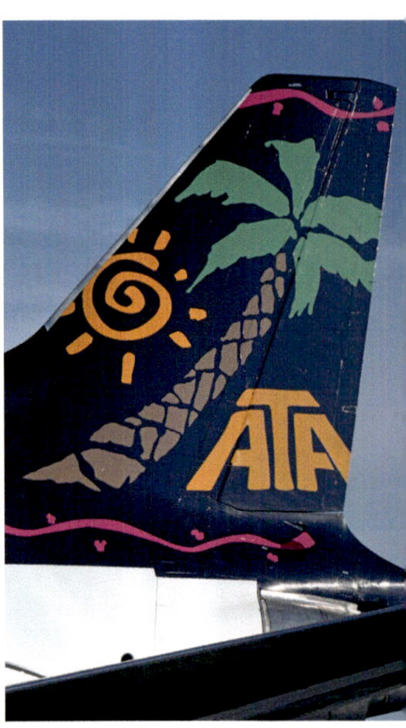

Above left: ATA's (American Trans Air) Lockheed L-1011-500 N162AT awaits further activity on the cargo ramp. While this airline was significantly involved with leisure travel (one of its advertising slogans was "On ATA, You're on Vacation"), much of its presence at BWI in this time period involved military charters for the U.S. government. Prior to ATA's usage, the airplane had flown for Royal Jordanian Airlines.

Above right: Present duties notwithstanding, N162AT's tail decorations implied fun, and relaxation; that is a long way from camouflage!

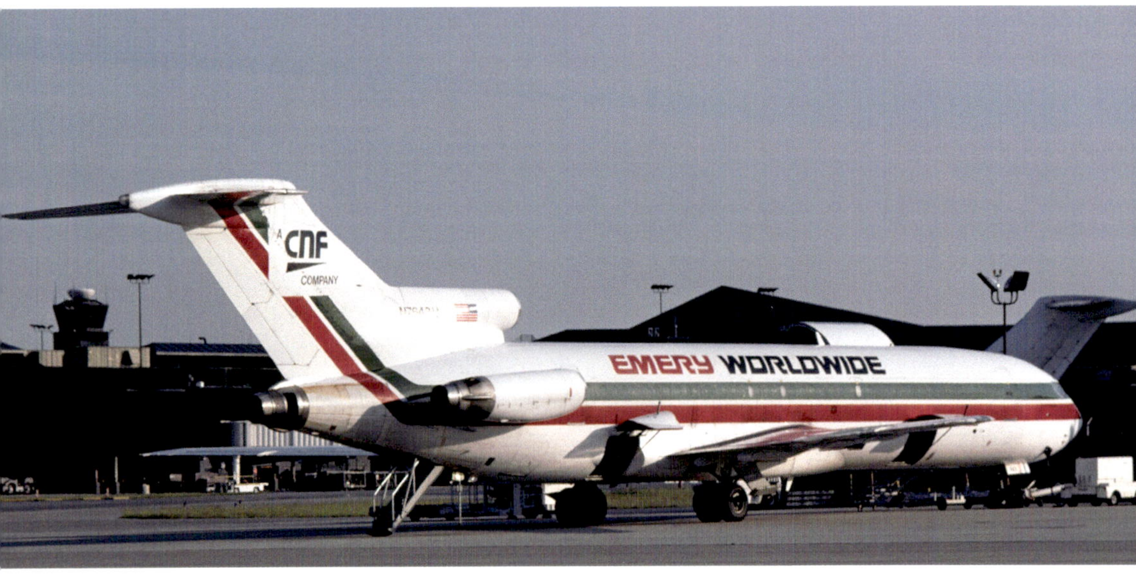

Here is the other side of Emery's N7643U, with the BWI tower on the terminal in the background.

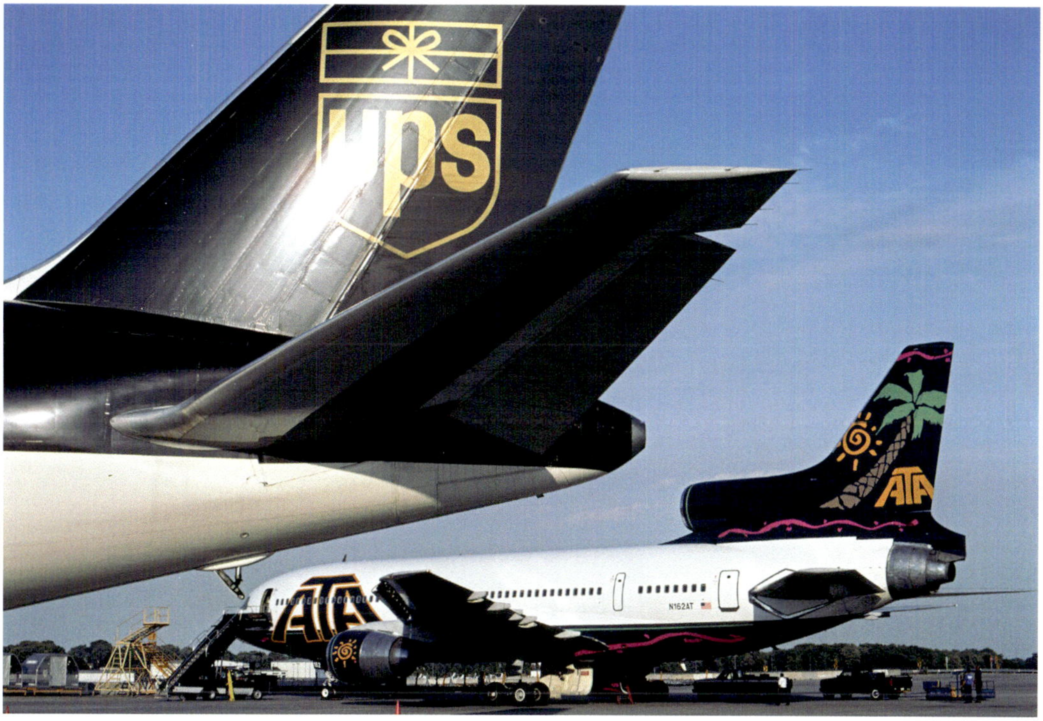

ATA's L-1011 was parked nearby the UPS 767-300, N312UP, that we saw earlier.

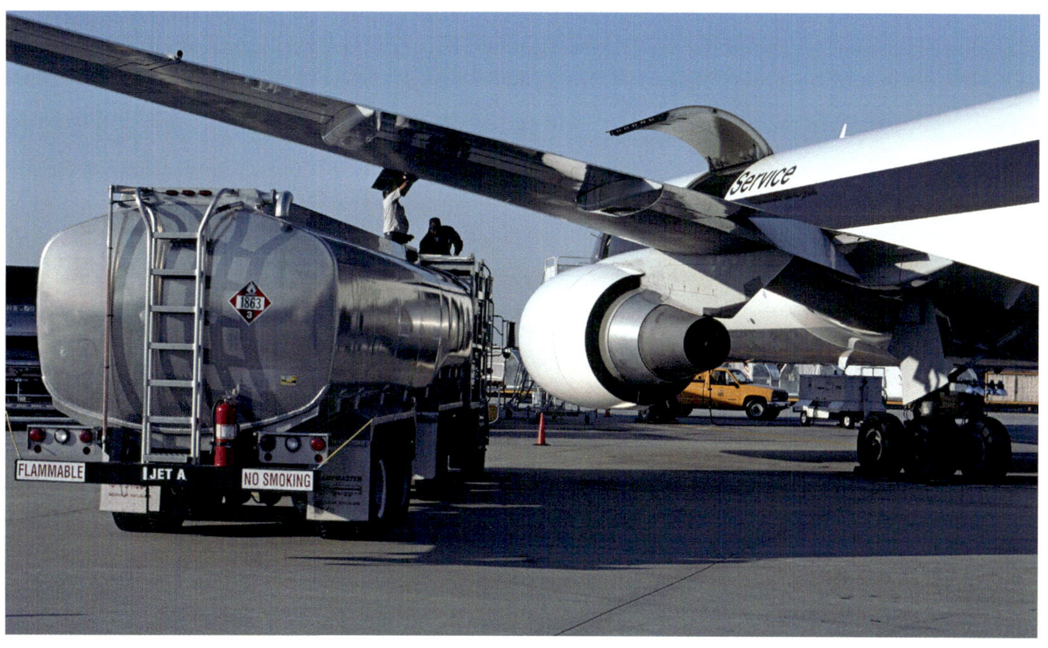

Now N312UP is about to take on a fuel load for tonight's mission.

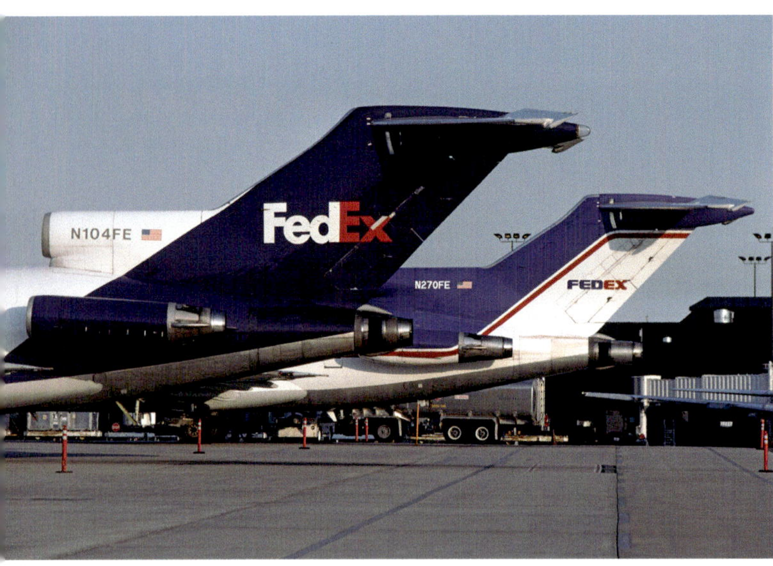

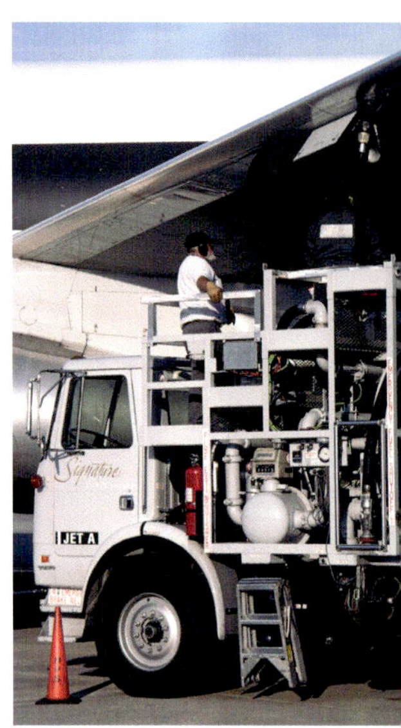

Above left: A pair of 727s from UPS' principal competitor, FedEx, are also awaiting later-evening activities. N270FE, a -200 model, is in the older livery, featuring a brighter shade of purple, while closer to the camera, N104FE, a 727-100, is in the newer, dark purple livery.

Above right: Back at N312UP, fuel is now flowing into the aircraft's wing tanks.

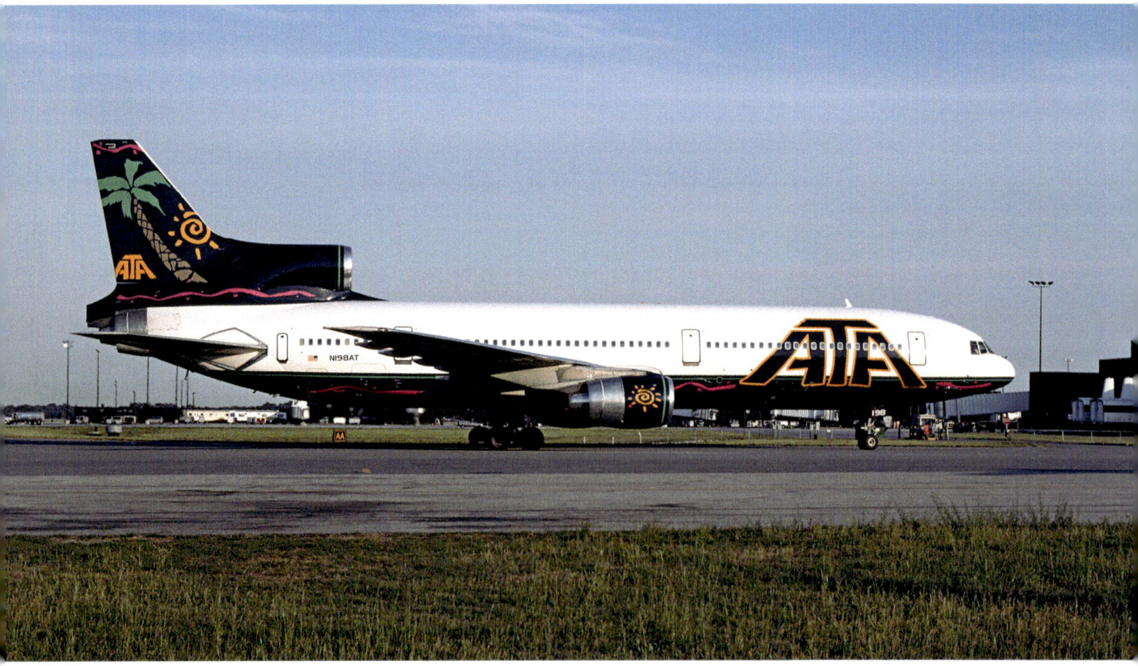

The sun is now lower in the sky, and N198AT, a "full-sized" -100 model of the L-1011 is taxiing towards the international terminal.

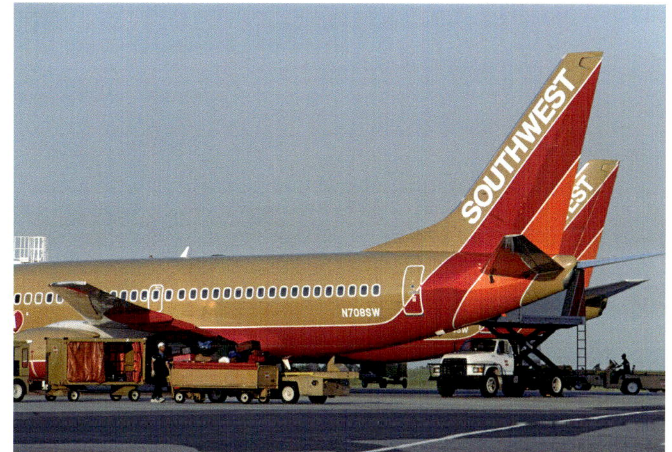

Baggage is ready for loading adjacent to Southwest 737-700 N708SW; on the other side of the aircraft, the rear galley is being serviced.

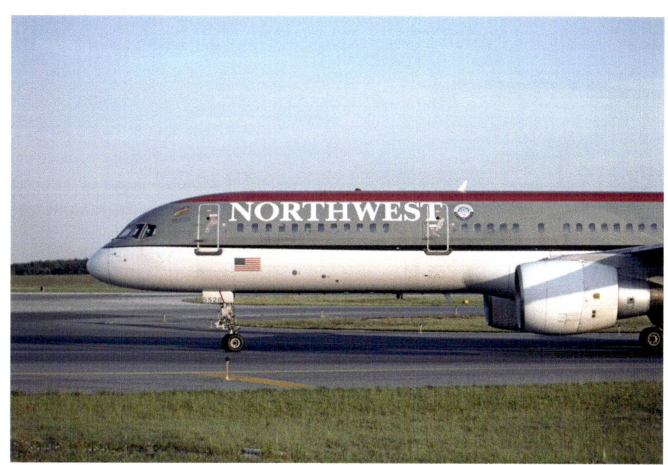

N528US, a Northwest 757, taxies by, with markings celebrating the airline's fiftieth anniversary of trans-Pacific service, as well as its "airline alliance" with KLM Royal Dutch Airlines.

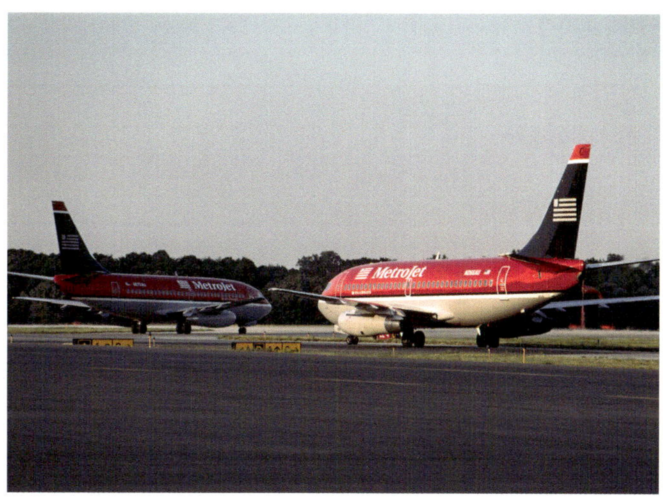

A pair of MetroJet 737s (N272AU and N266AU) are both heading towards runway 28 departures.

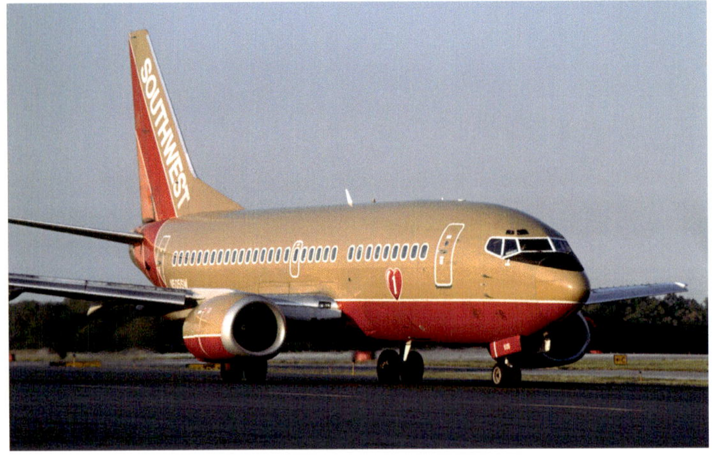

N505SW, a Southwest 737-500, looks like it is also ready to "get out of town."

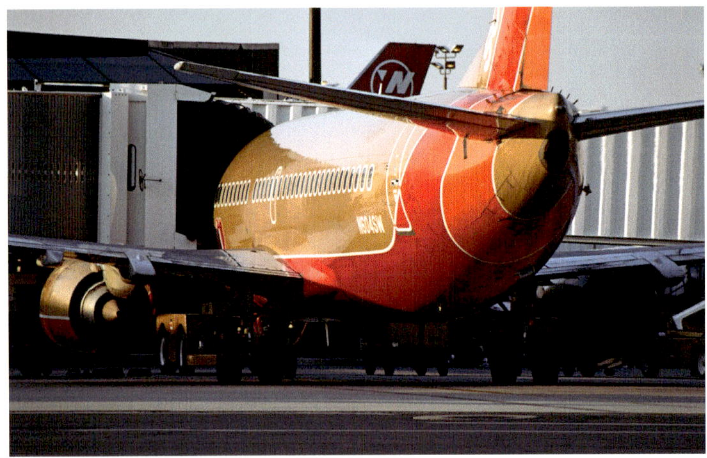

At the outer end of Concourse C, N604SW, a 737-300, appears to be buttoned-up and ready to leave the gate; that is the tail of a Northwest 757 in the background.

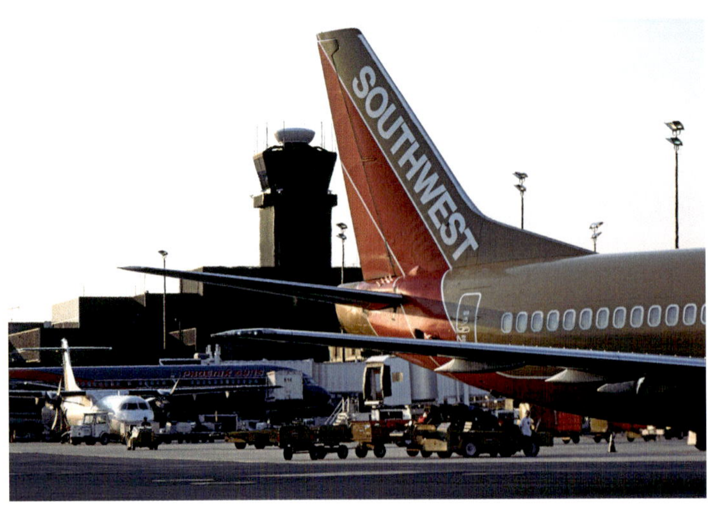

Looking back down Concourse C from the other side finds a Southwest 737-300 at its gate; a Continental Express ATR-42; and the America West 757 painted in the colors of the Phoenix Suns basketball team.

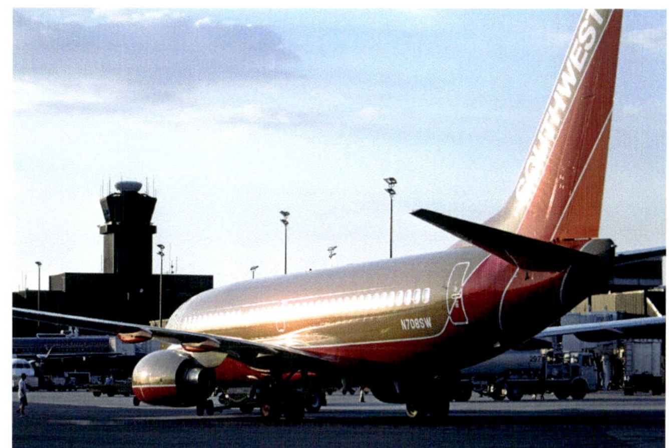

The lighting gets more dramatic as N708SW, a 737-700, catches the low light of the setting sun as it is being pushed back.

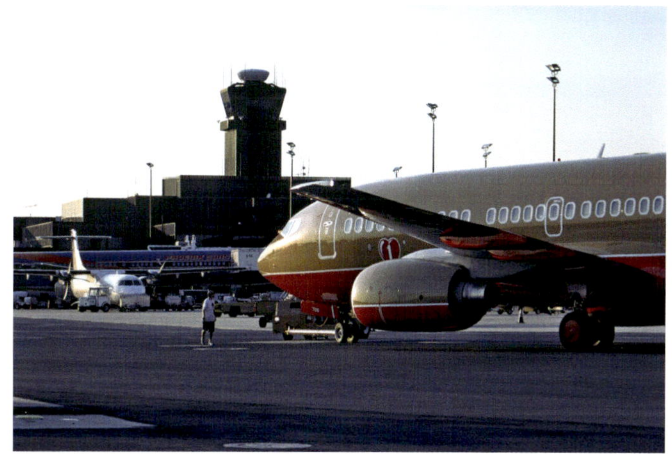

The glint on N708SW diminishes as the aircraft turns, with the aircraft's nose now illuminated.

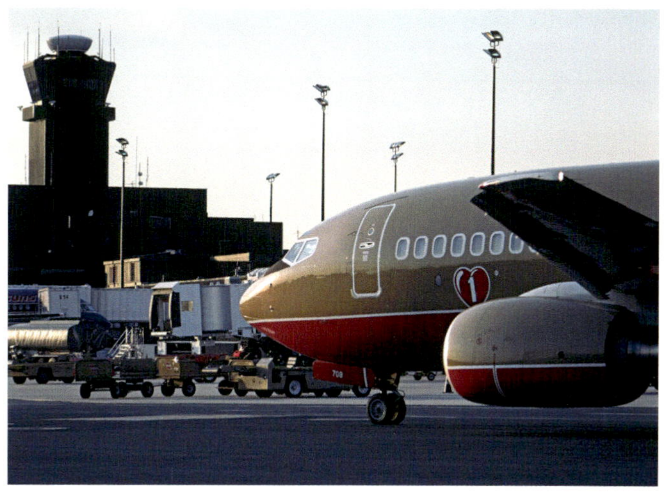

The tow bar is off, and N708SW is prepared to taxi away from the gate.

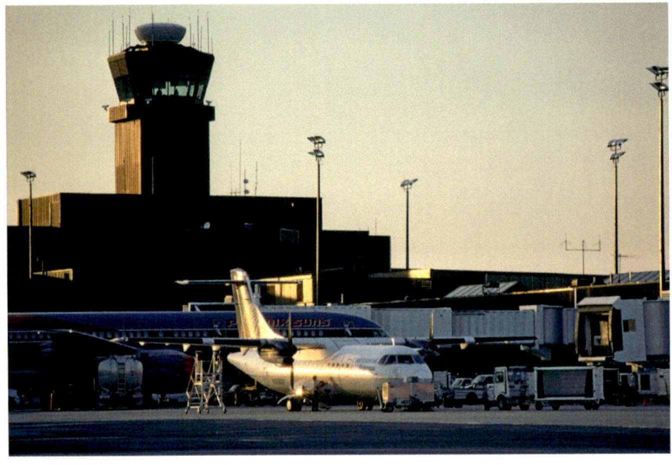

Now the Continental Express ATR-42, N21837, is lit nicely.

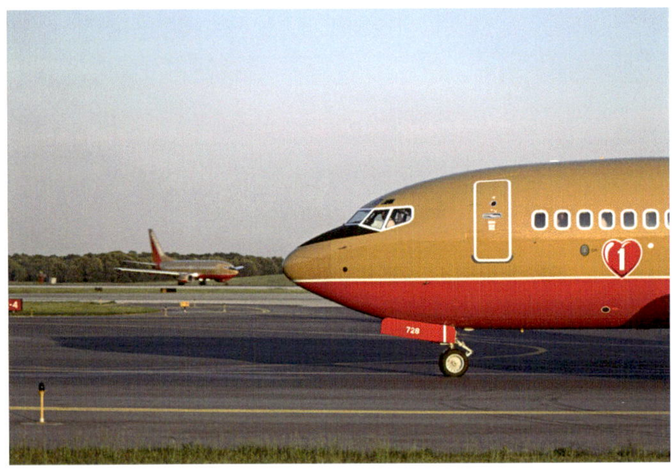

N728SW, another 737-700, is preparing to taxi to runway 28 for takeoff, where another Southwest 737 is on its takeoff roll.

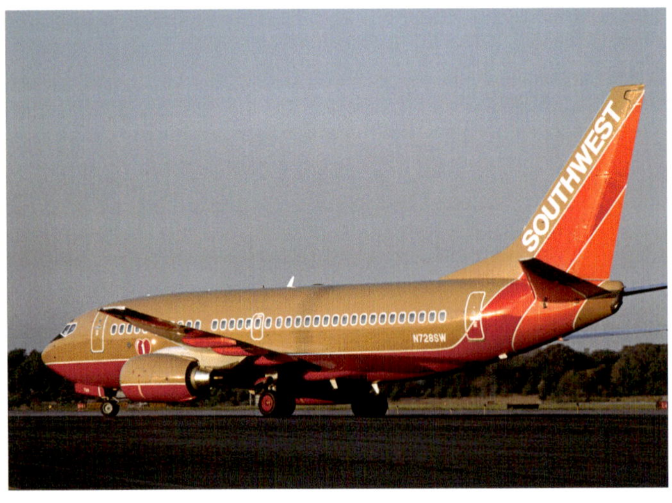

Now, N728SW heads east to 28 for its own departure.

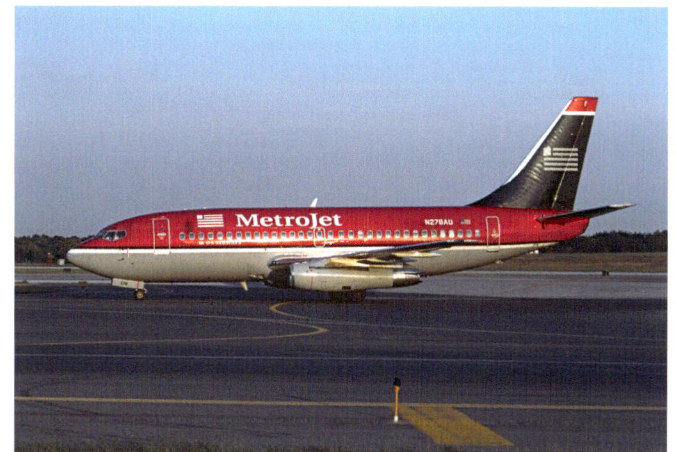

MetroJet's N278AU poses for its portrait as it prepares to follow thc two Southwest aircraft.

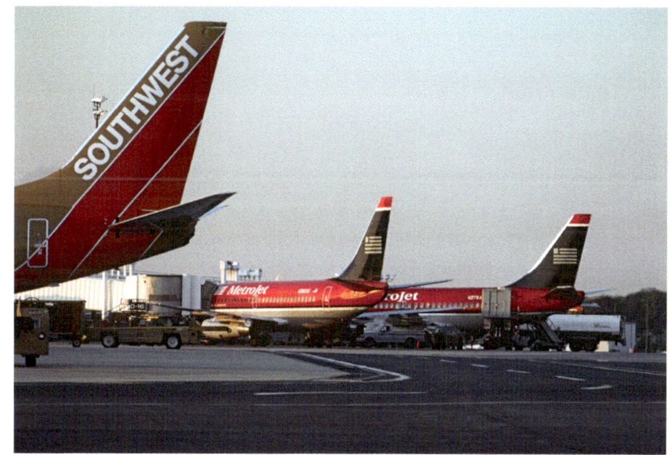

Other MetroJet 737-200s can be seen on Concourse D, along with the tail of a Southwest aircraft on the outer end of Concourse C.

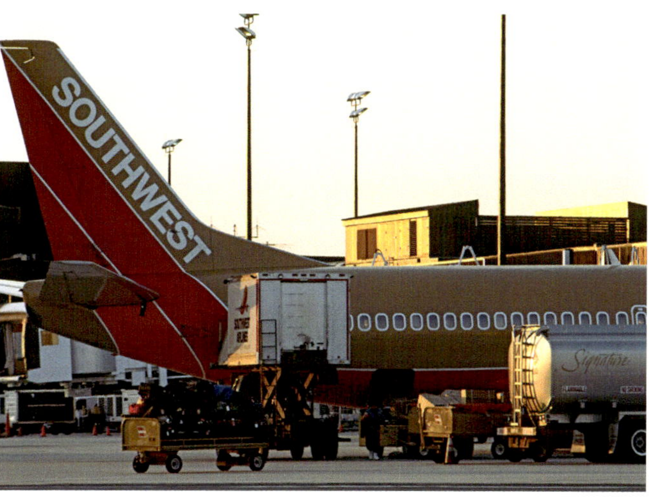

Lots of vehicles are addressing the needs of N659SW during its time at the gate.

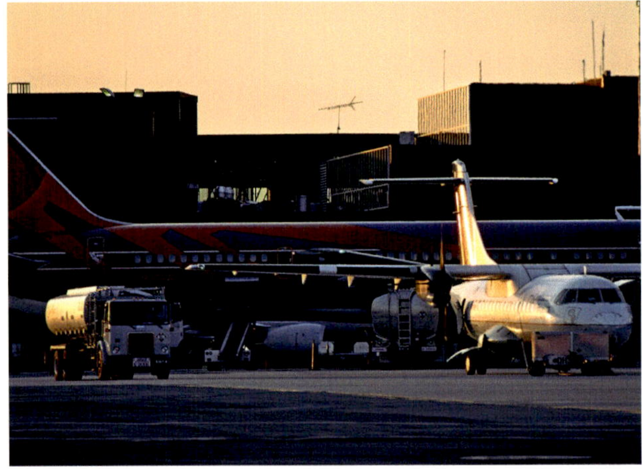

Most of the west side of Concourse C is no longer reached by what is left of the day's sunlight, but the Continental Express ATR-42 and the fuel truck to its left are making good use of what little sunlight remains.

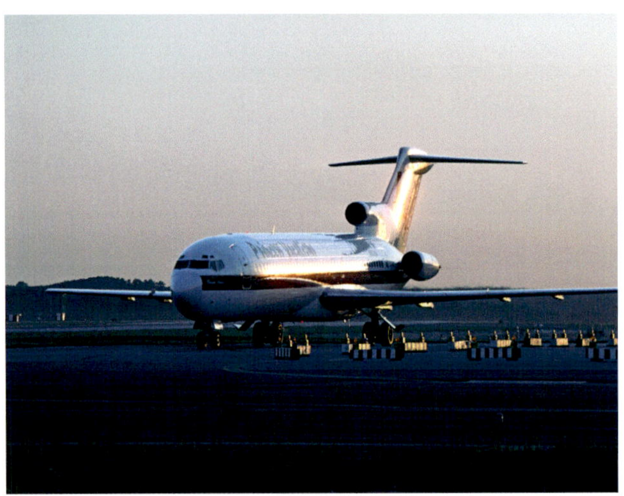

Glinting from the setting sun, N552NA of L.B. Limited, previously known as Laker Airways (Bahamas), Ltd., a 727-200 delivered to PSA (Pacific Southwest Airlines) for intra-California services, is heading for the gate with its load of passengers likely returning from a "sun and fun" vacation experience in accordance with its "Princess Vacations" titles. In addition to these two carriers, it also flew for Sterling Airways of Denmark; Mexicana; and Mexican airline Aerolineas Internacionales.

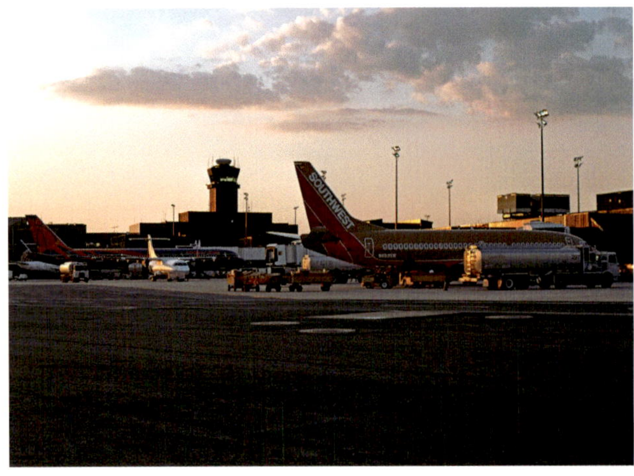

Taking a wider look at Concourse C's west side provides this serene view of the continuing activity on the ramp as daylight ends.

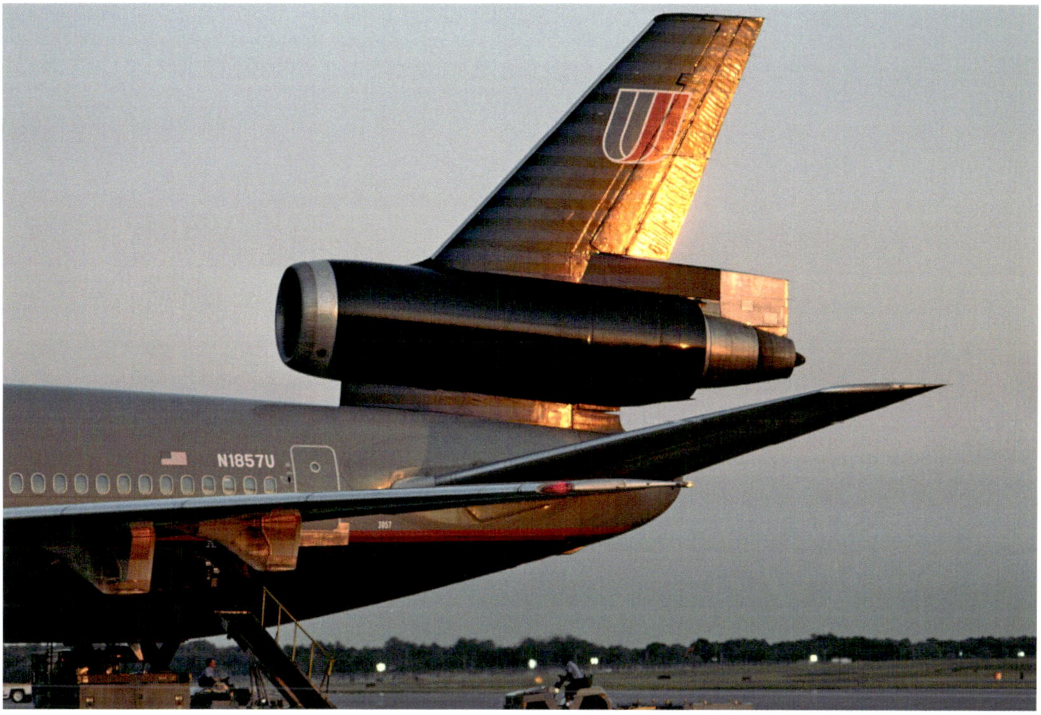

Over on its gate, United's DC-10 N1857U is also catching the last rays of sunlight. This suggests that it might be a good idea for us to take a look at what has been happening out by the runways.

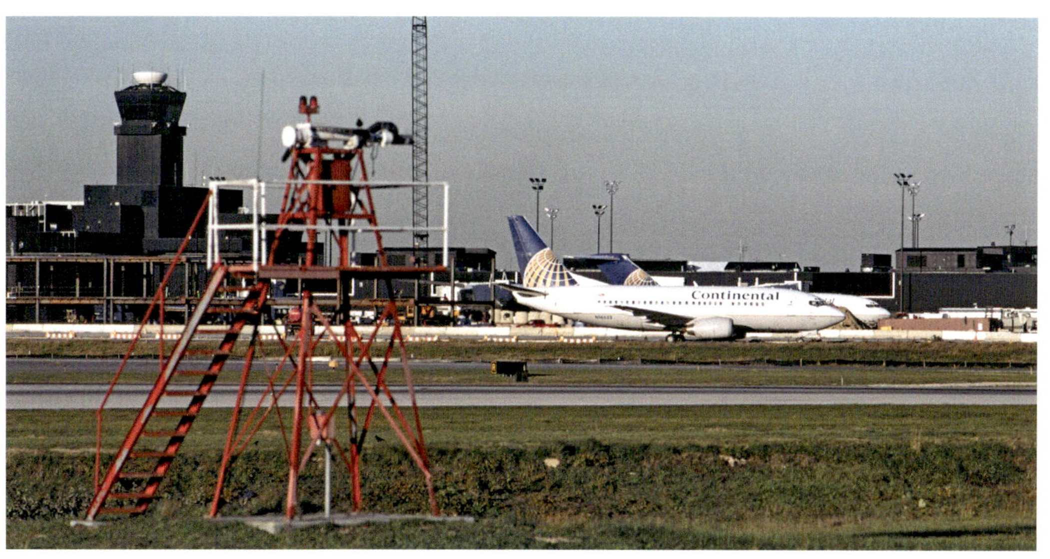

Our new vantage point is adjacent to the BWI Fire/Rescue station located south of runway 10-28, and west of runway 15R/33L. Takeoffs are occurring on 28, and landings on 33L. This view looks back at the terminal and Concourse C; two Continental aircraft (N16632, a 737-500, and an unidentified 727-200) are taxiing by.

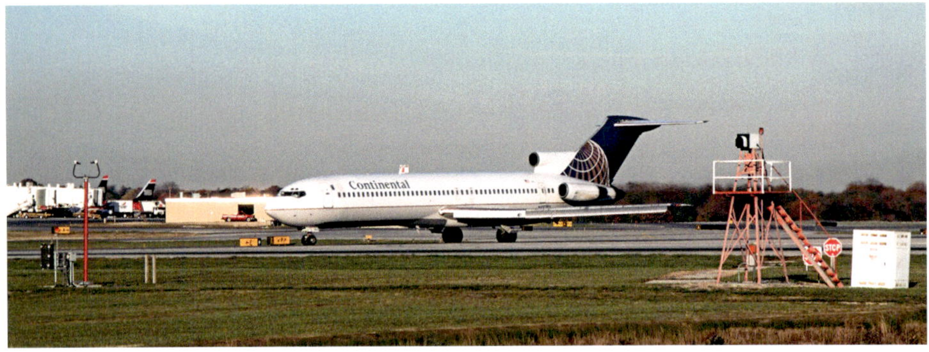

Continental's 727-200 N45793 is accelerating along runway 28 on its takeoff roll, and it will be airborne shortly.

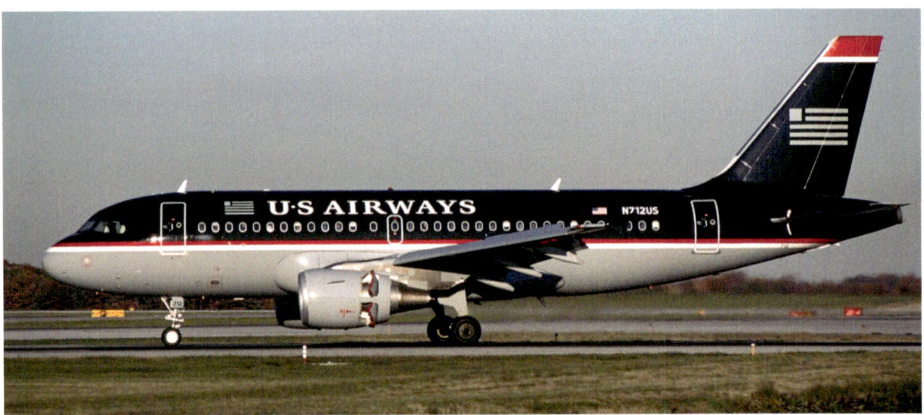

US Airways A319 N712US has landed on runway 33L, and it is using reverse thrust to slow the aircraft prior to exiting the runway and taxiing to its gate.

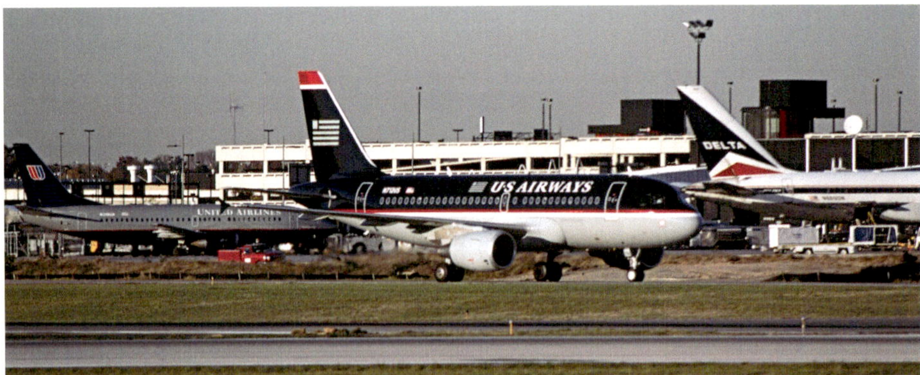

After turning off runway 33L, N712US has made a 180-degree turn, and is taxiing parallel to the runway on its way to a Concourse D gate. Seen in the background are a United 737-300 and a Delta 757.

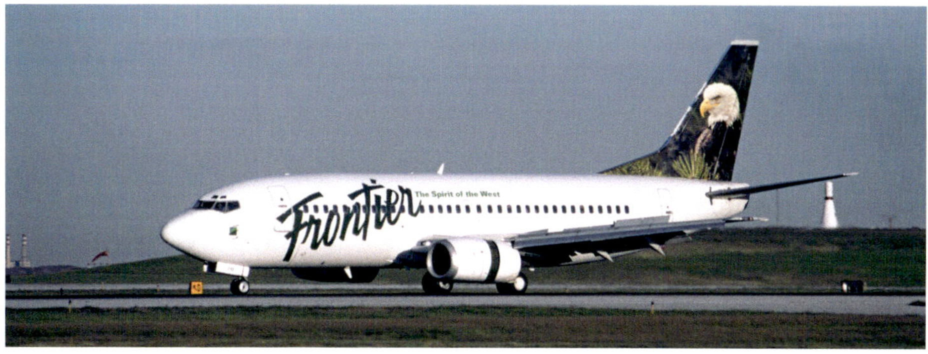

Frontier's 737-300 N310FL is slowing following its landing on 33L; that is a stern-looking visage of the bald eagle depicted on the tail!

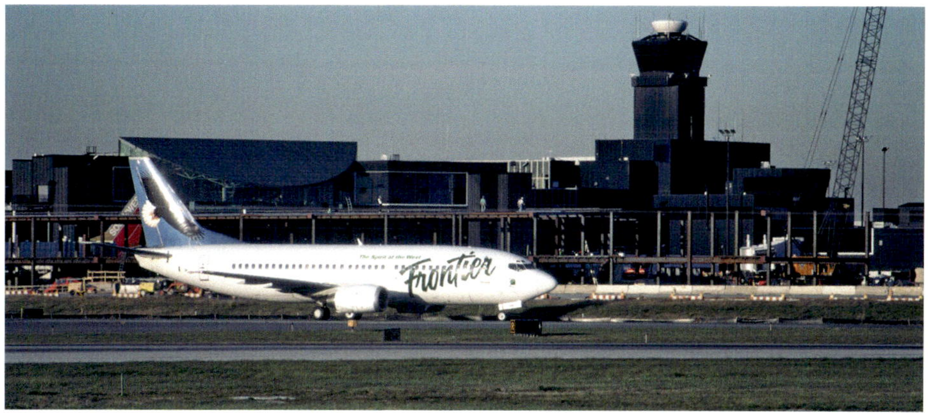

The other side of N310FL depicts a bald eagle in flight; seen as it continues to taxi parallel to 33L.

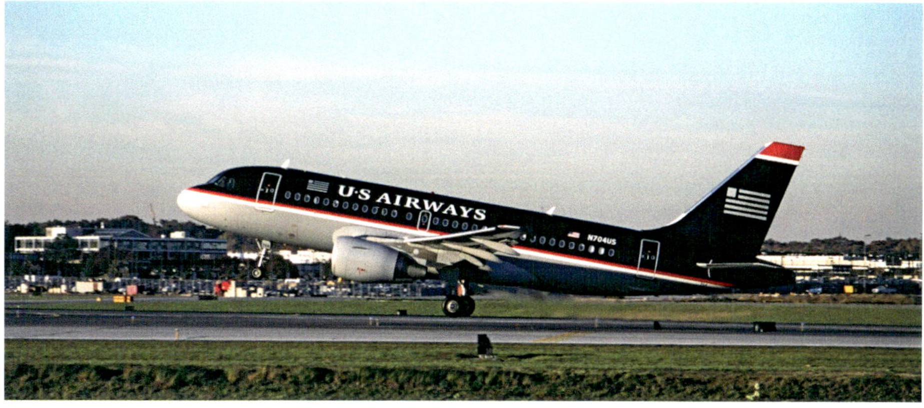

N704US, a US Airways A319, has rotated, and is about to depart the ground as it takes off on runway 28.

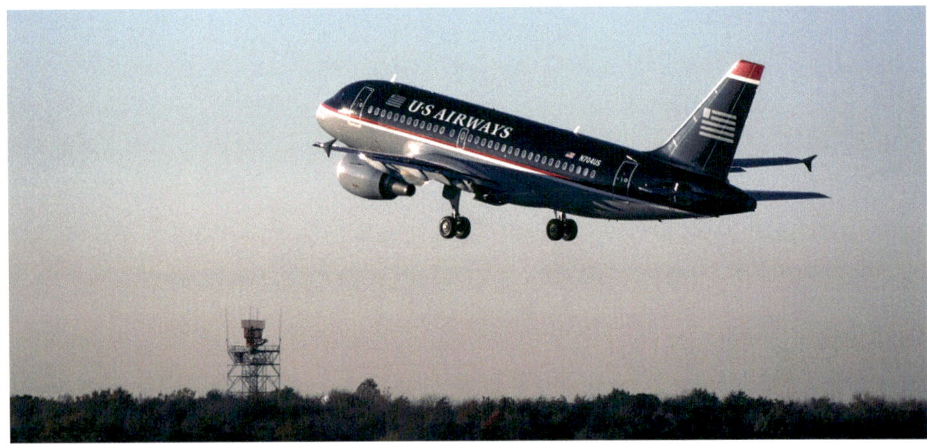

Now N704US is climbing out into the setting sun.

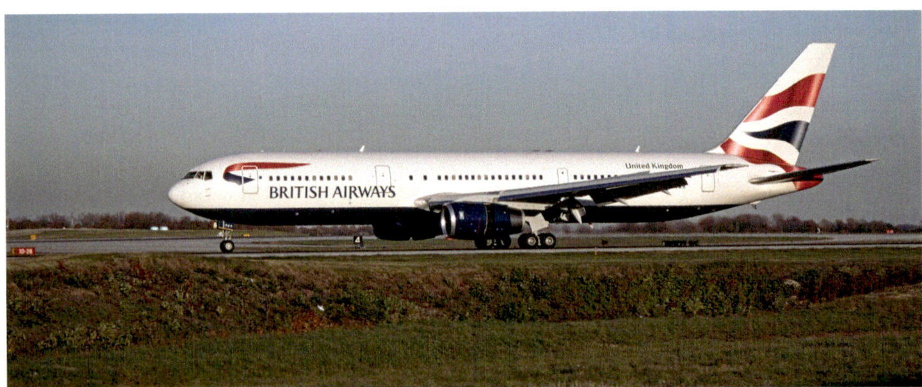

Here we see British Airways 767-300 G-BNWR again, this time arriving from London on runway 33L.

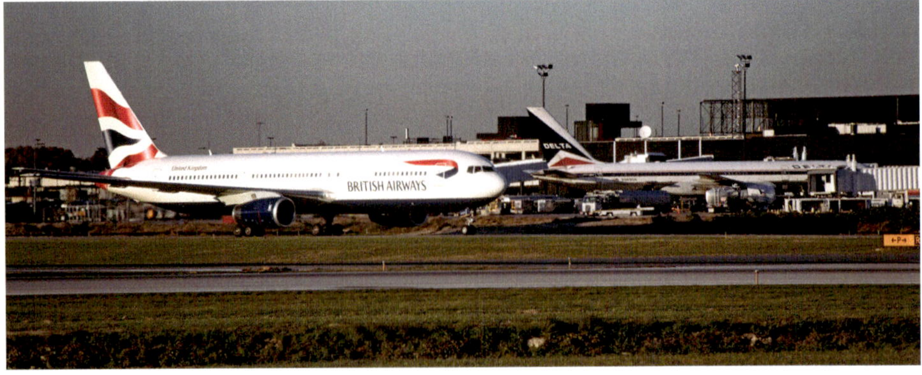

A look at the other side of "Whiskey Romeo" as it begins its relatively long taxi to a Concourse E gate.

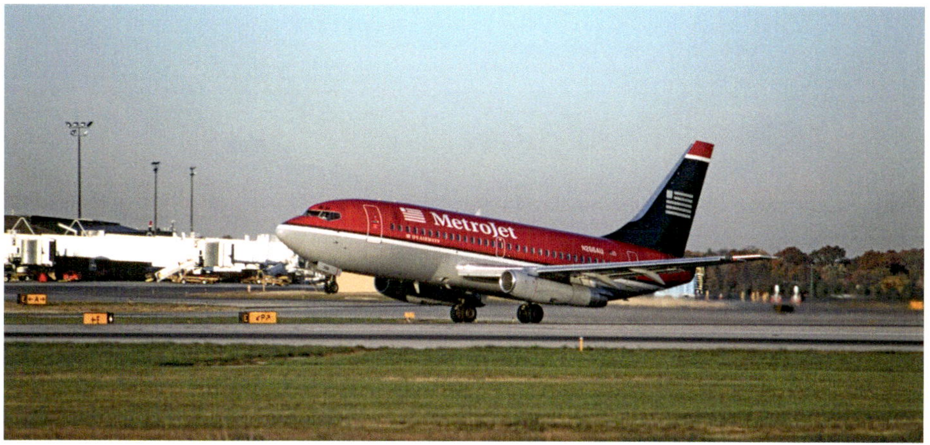

MetroJet N266AU is rotating on runway 28 just short of the intersection with 15R/33L.

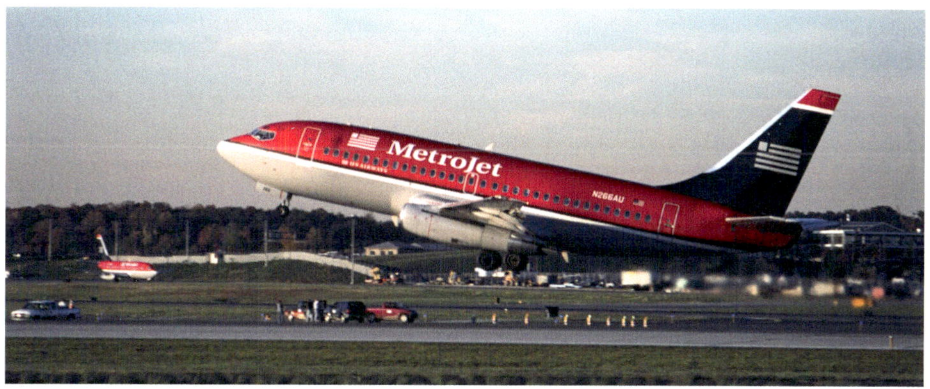

West of the intersection, N266AU is airborne, with another 737-200 in the same livery visible in the distance.

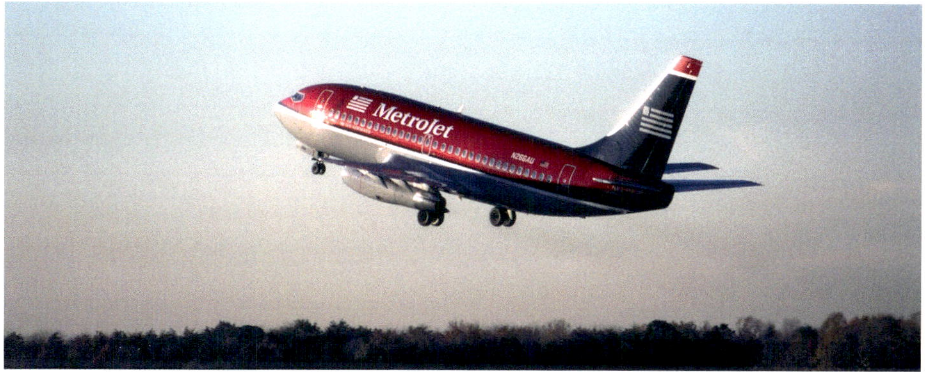

Climbing out above runway 28, the landing gear on N266AU will be retracting shortly.

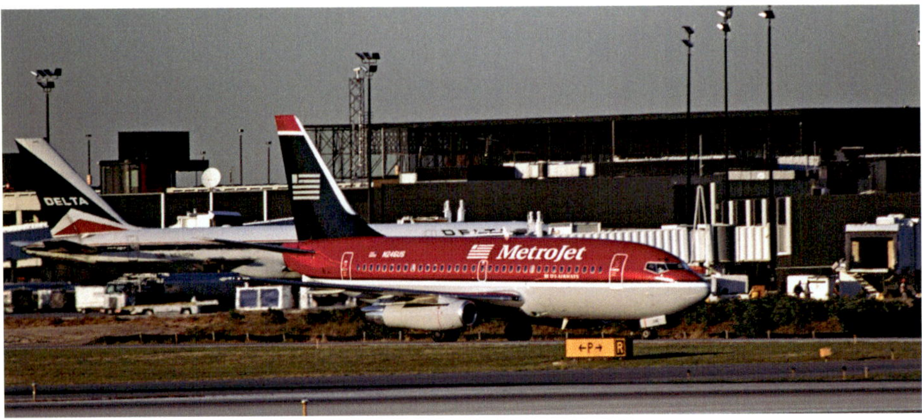

N246US, another MetroJet 737-200, taxies on its way to Concourse D.

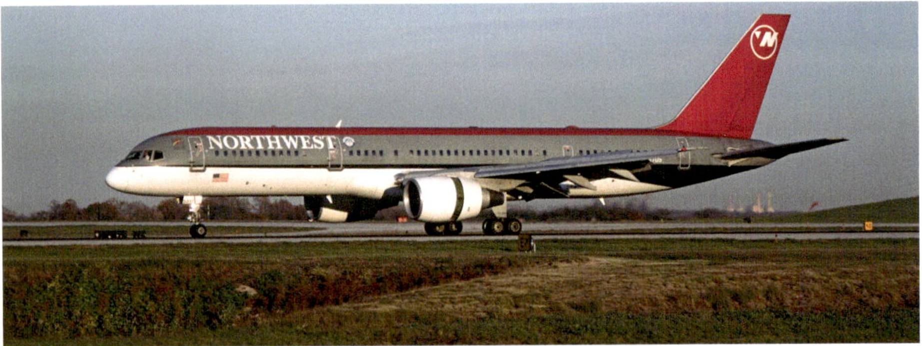

Northwest 757 N517US is utilizing reverse thrust to slow the aircraft following its landing on runway 33L.

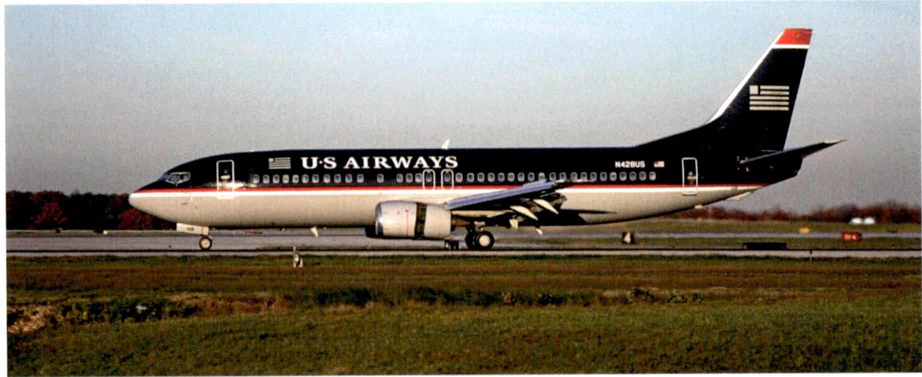

The same feature (reverse thrust) is being applied to US Airways' 737-400 N428US as it follows the Northwest 757. The 737-400 is the largest of what are referred to as the "Classics" in the 737 family, the -300/-400/-500; interestingly the -500 is the smallest of the three types, the higher number reflecting that it followed the other two models into the market, timewise.

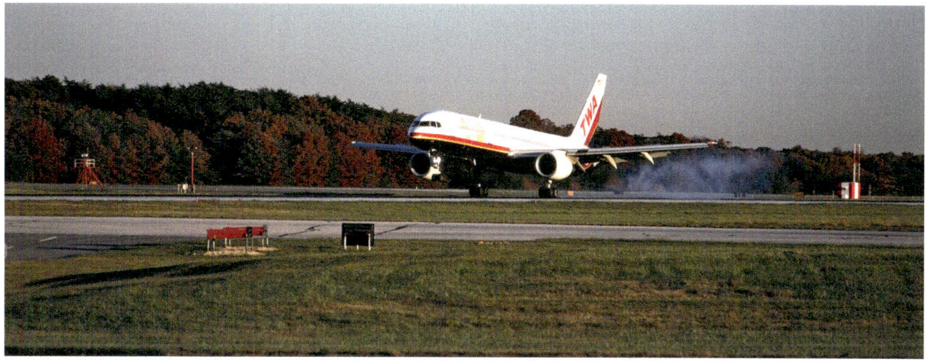

Unlike automobiles, where "burning rubber" typically takes place as the vehicle starts, the aircraft version occurs at the end of the flight, as seen here when TWA 757 N716TW comes back into contact with the ground as it lands on runway 33L.

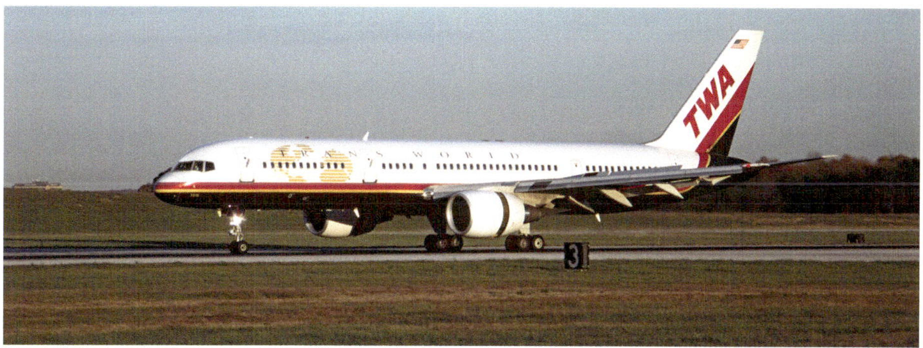

The nose gear on N716TW catches some "glint light" reflection from the sun while the thrust reversers slow the aircraft as it approaches the intersection with runway 10-28.

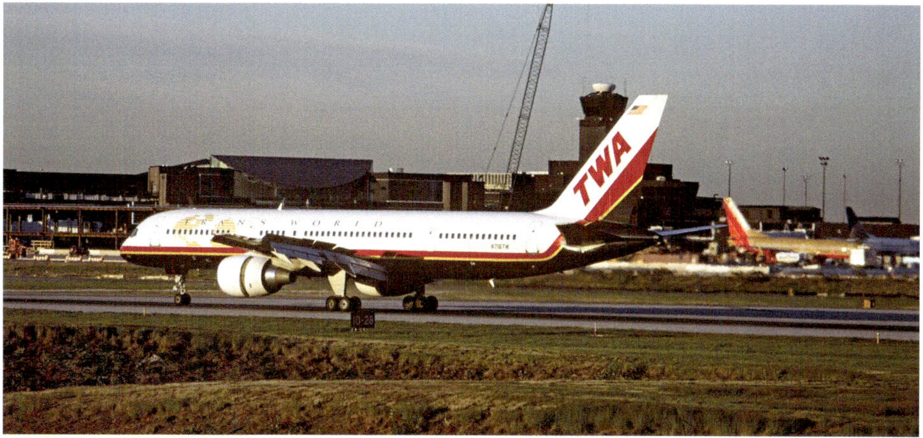

N716TW is in TWA's final paint scheme, featuring a bold take on the national colors of red, white, and blue, along with a gold stripe.

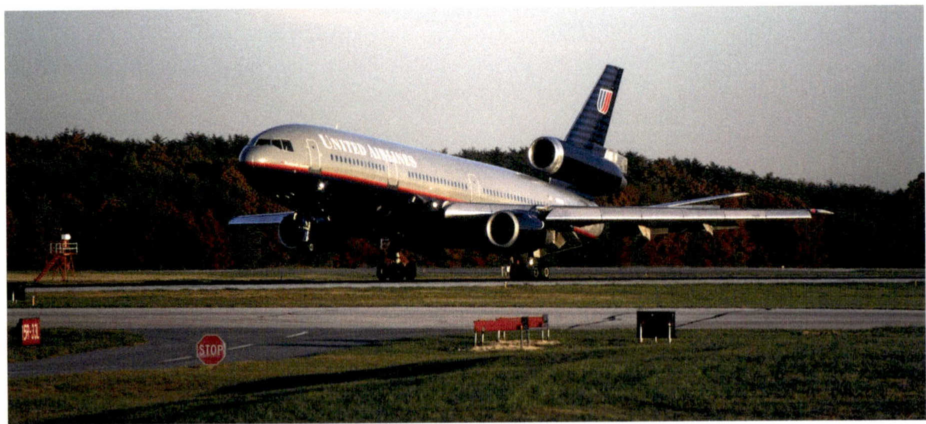

Next landing on runway 33L is this DC-10 of United, N1849U, which already has its main landing gear firmly on the ground.

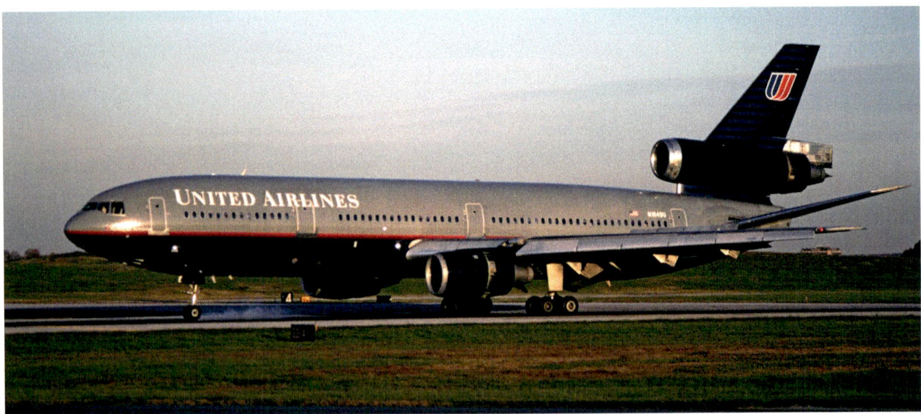

The touchdown of N1849U's nosewheel provides a modest amount of blue smoke from the tires, however.

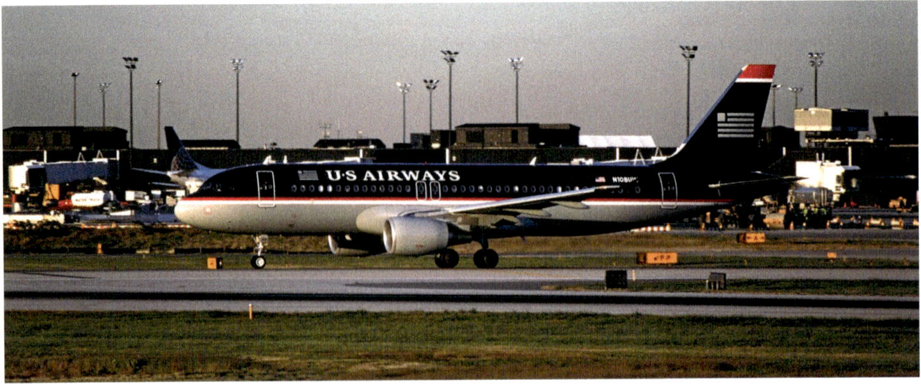

US Airways A320 N108UW is departing to the west on runway 28.

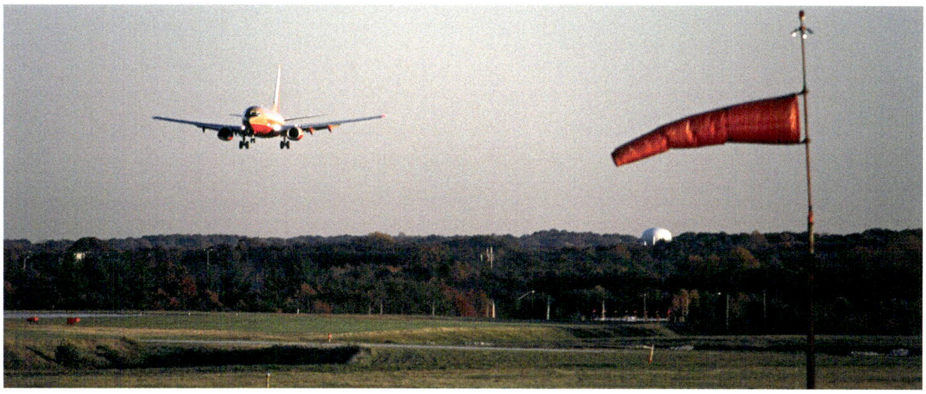

N734SA, a Southwest 737-700, is on "short final" to land on runway 33L, heading northwest. The windsock on the right indicates that the wind is coming from a more westerly direction, which is why takeoffs are occurring on runway 28.

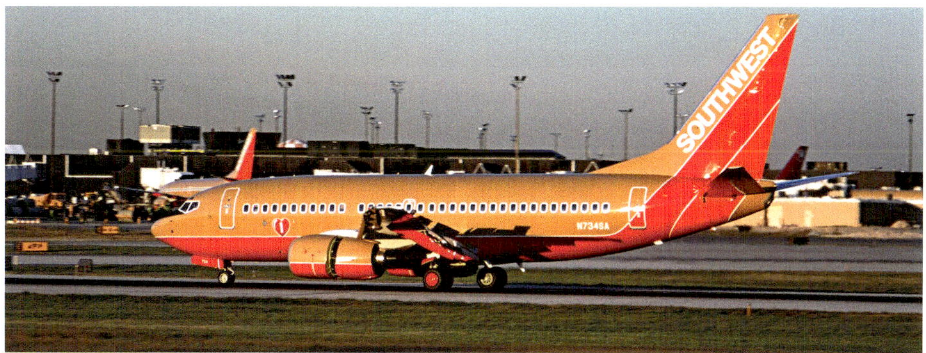

N734SA has now returned to the earth, as the engine reversers slow its velocity; the light is getting gorgeous as sunset nears. The angle of the light is also useful for displaying the complexity of the aircraft's wing structure, including the various "high-lift" devices utilized for landings and takeoffs.

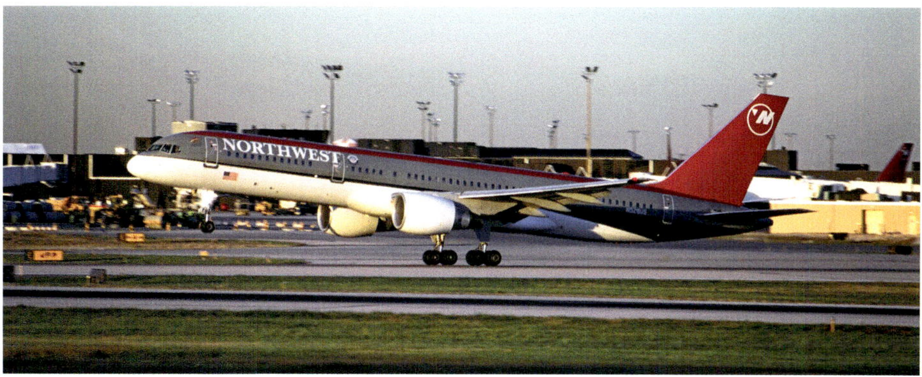

Another nose-gear glint reflection, as Northwest 757 N508US rotates on its way down runway 28.

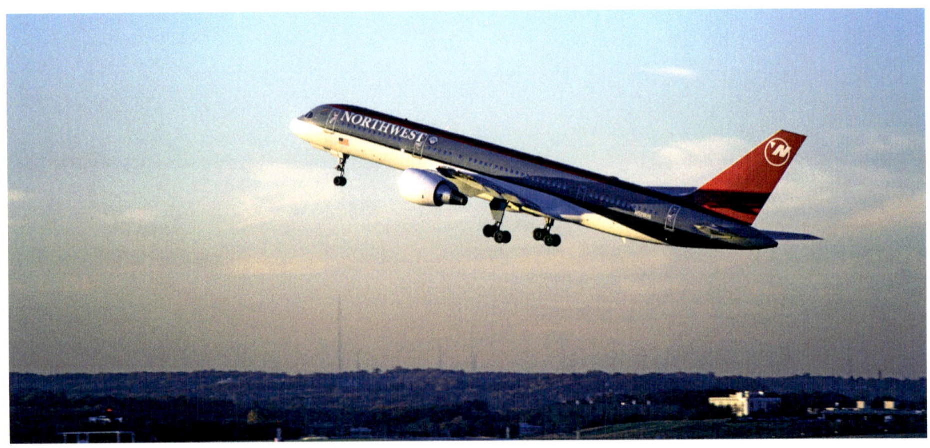

N508US exhibits the robust performance of the 757 as it climbs out into the sunset.

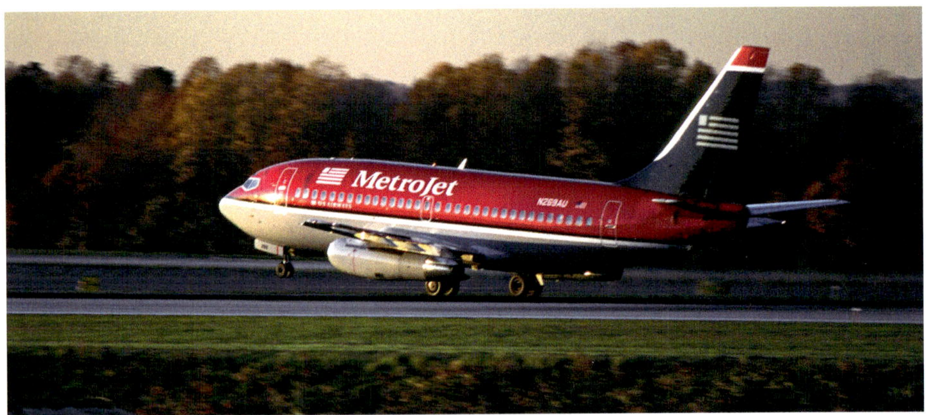

N269AU, another MetroJet 737-200, follows the Northwest 757, as it too departs on runway 28.

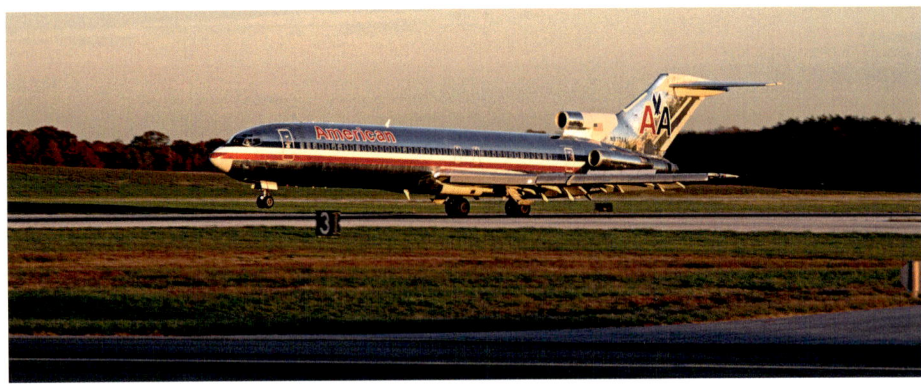

Next up is an American Airlines 727-200, N870AA, which has just touched down on runway 33L.

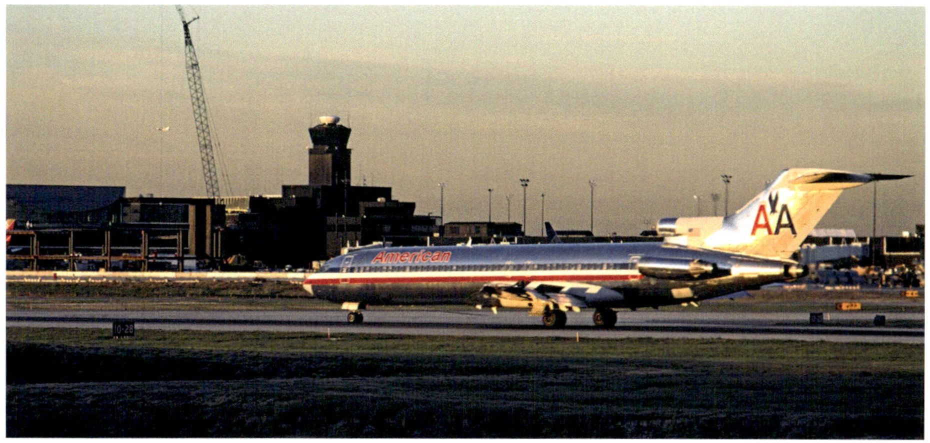

The mostly bare-metal 727 slows so that it can access Concourse C.

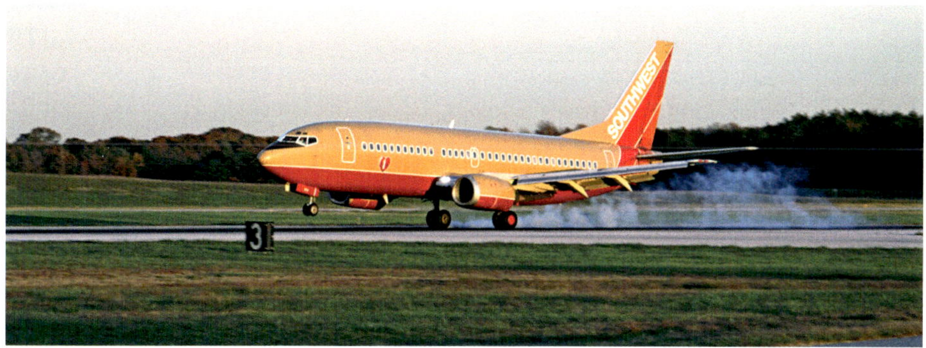

N374SW, a 737-300, has planted its main gear "feet" firmly on runway 33L, confirmed by significant visual evidence.

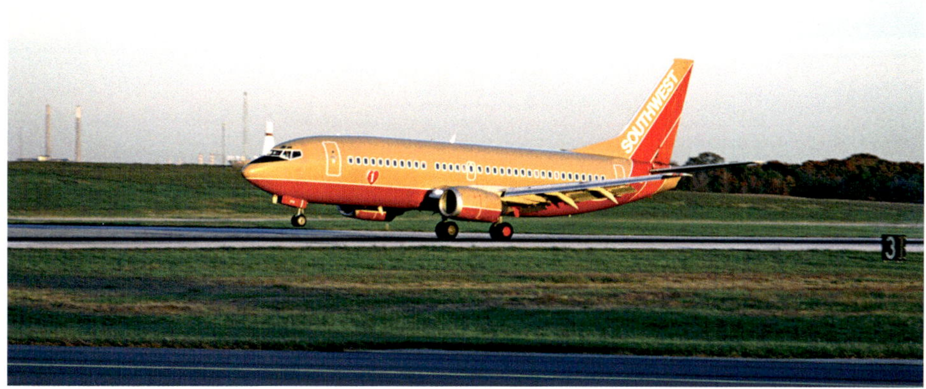

A few seconds later, however, the 'evidence' of the firm landing has been left behind, even before the nose gear has touched down.

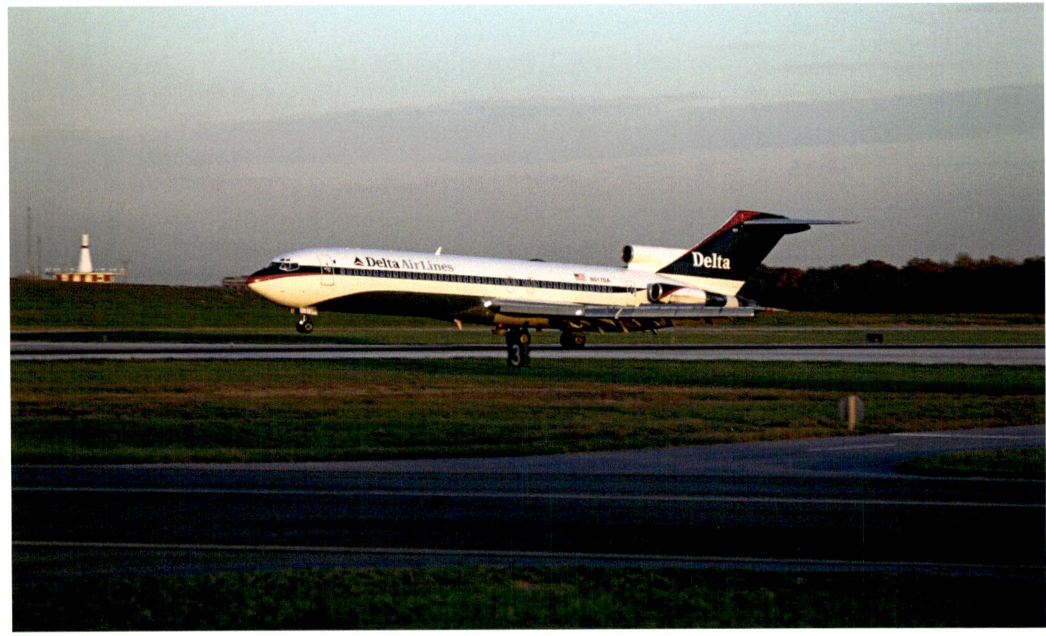

Delta's 727-200 N517DA is next in the landing queue.

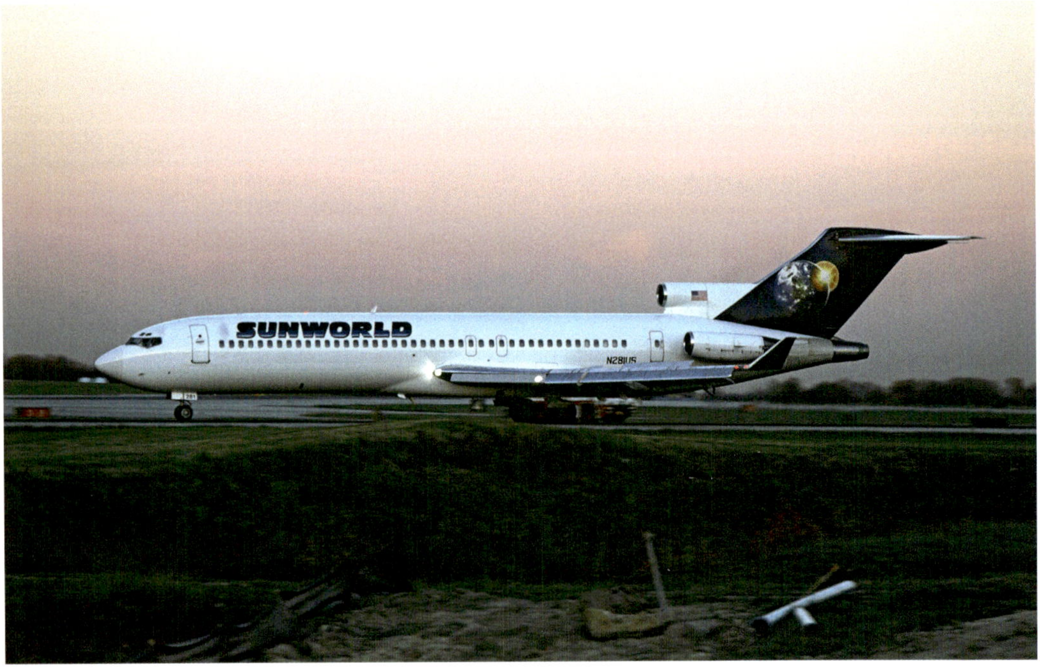

Daylight is disappearing rapidly as Sunworld International Airlines' 727-200 with winglets, a former Northwest Airlines aircraft, lands on runway 33L. Accordingly, it is time for us to return to the terminal area to check out what goes on after the natural light is "turned off" for the evening.

4
At the Twilight's Last Gleaming, and Beyond

Depending on the season, as the late-day peak concludes, so does the natural light. While fleeting, this can be one of the best times to be airside, from a visual perspective. The evening's golden glow reflects off the continuing competitive struggle until it becomes difficult to discern what is happening on the ramp from inside the terminal.

Outside, however, a different form of entertainment is in place, featuring a multi-hued light show. Not quite up to Christmas decoration standards, but colorful in a functional way. Some of the lights, such as aircraft marker beacons, were there all day, but little noticed. Now, they have a bolder presence, as do the tails of aircraft which are illuminated to display the company colors. Most of the passengers will see little of the show, but a few will get exposed to the night's magic as they cross the ramp to board their aircraft.

By now, the rare tropical birds have returned from their sunspot destinations to roost before working again the next morning so that others (travelers) can play. Other aircraft have arrived from more mundane locations to become RON (Remain Over Night) aircraft, while a few will turn back for a late evening trip either to the far coast, or a twenty-four-hour attraction such as Las Vegas.

The freighters are finally in their element, as the airport's ultimate late-risers are readied for their high-priority missions. Cargo which has been collected and consolidated during the afternoon and evening arrives via a parade of trucks. No fancy terminals, with creature comforts and concessions, here; everything is purposeful and geared to accomplishing loading in as little time as possible.

After all, some of this traffic carries a money-back guarantee that it will be at the intended destination by the appointed time the next morning, or else! Human strength and sweat are employed where applicable, but the bulk of the loads require mechanized assistance. While the cargo ramp may have been quiet during the day, a palpable sense of urgency is present now: keep the loader fully occupied; get the doors shut; and dispatch the aircraft on schedule.

Finally, late in the evening, activity reverts to near static, with the occasional late arrival and routine overnight maintenance punctuating the calmness. In a relatively short time, however, the day shift will return to the pre-dawn darkness, and the airside's daily cycle will begin anew.

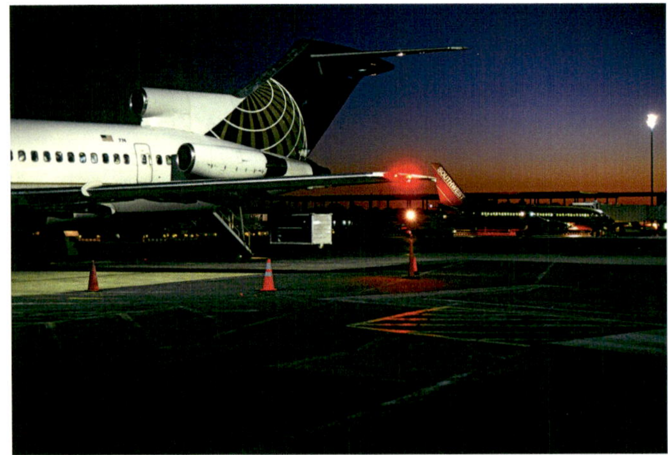

The last orange glow is in the sky as we stand on Concourse C's ramp. In view are Continental's 727-200 N15774 and a Southwest 737.

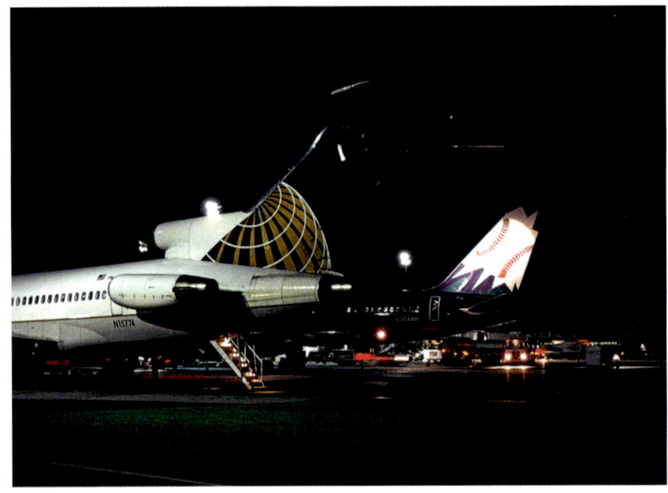

Looking down Concourse C reveals America West's 757 N904AW, in its Arizona Diamondbacks paint scheme.

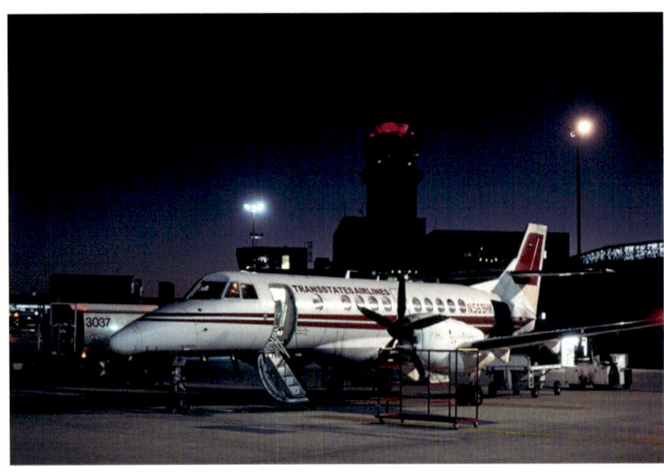

Not surprisingly, given the paint scheme, Trans States Airlines' BAe Jetstream 41 N569HK provides regional services for TWA.

Here is a wider view of the area the Trans States turboprop is parked in; some of the passengers in gate hold rooms have a view of this scene, albeit from a lower vantage point than our location.

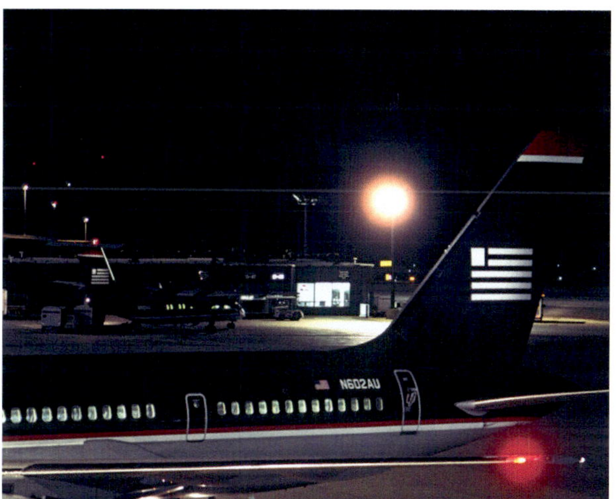

Over on Concourse D, we have a view of US Airways equipment, both mainline, in the form of 757 N602AU, and regional, US Airways Express Dash 8 N910HA of affiliate Piedmont Airlines. Previously, Piedmont had been Henson Aviation/Airlines, hence the initials in the registration. In 1963, Henson participated in one of the first "commuter replacement" deals with US Airways' predecessor Allegheny Airlines, for service between Hagerstown, Maryland, and Baltimore, a precursor of the modern regional airline industry.

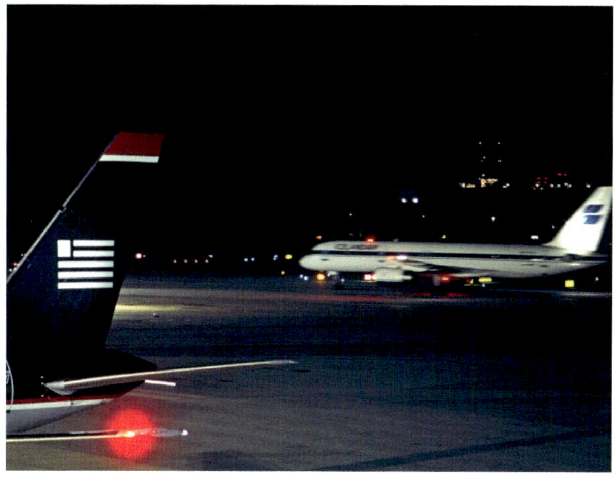

A meeting of 757s as Icelandair passes N602AU.

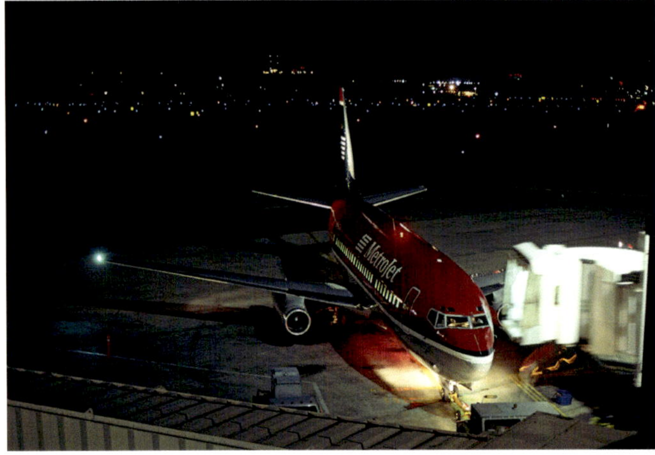

This MetroJet is "buttoned-up" and the boarding bridge is pulling away from the aircraft as it prepares to depart.

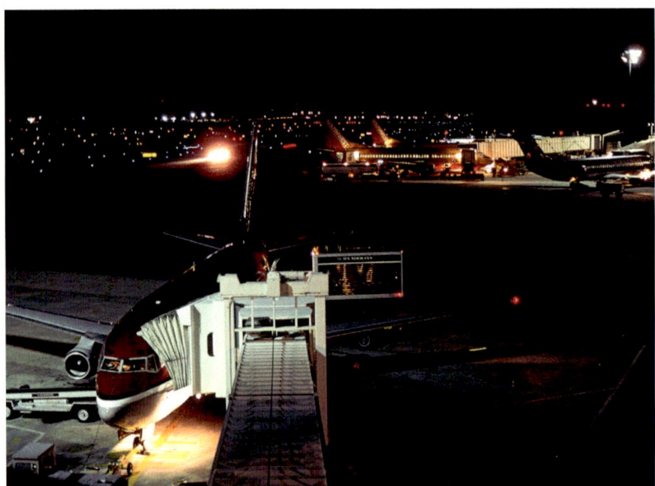

The view looking from the roof of Concourse D back towards the south end of Concourse C includes a MetroJet 737 in the foreground with a pair of Southwest 737s and a Northwest DC-9 behind. That is quite a light show in the background!

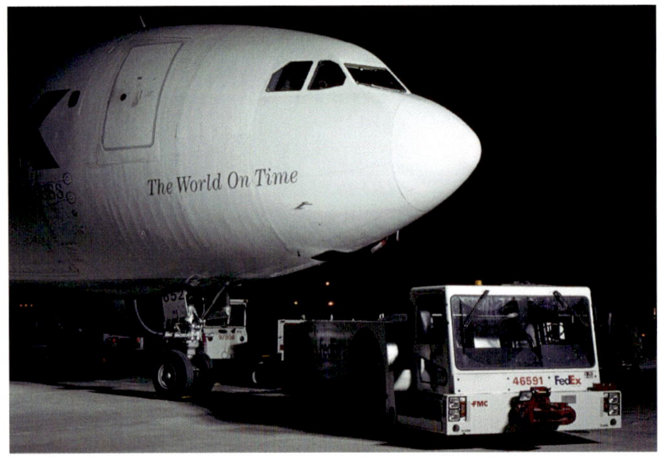

Over on the cargo ramp, activity is picking up, although this FedEx A300-600F, N652FE, currently is still at rest.

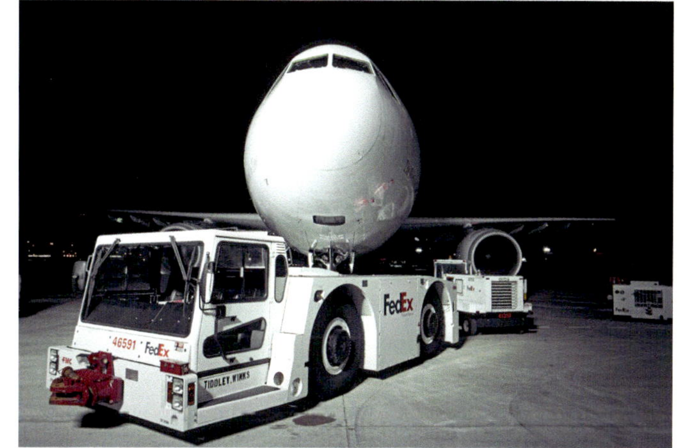

Current lack of activity notwithstanding, N652FE already has some ground equipment, including the pushback vehicle, in place.

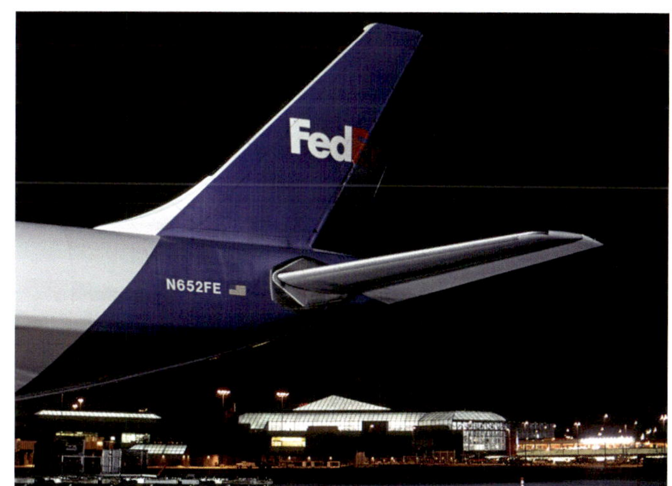

Behind this FedEx A300, there is a view of the brightly lit passenger facilities.

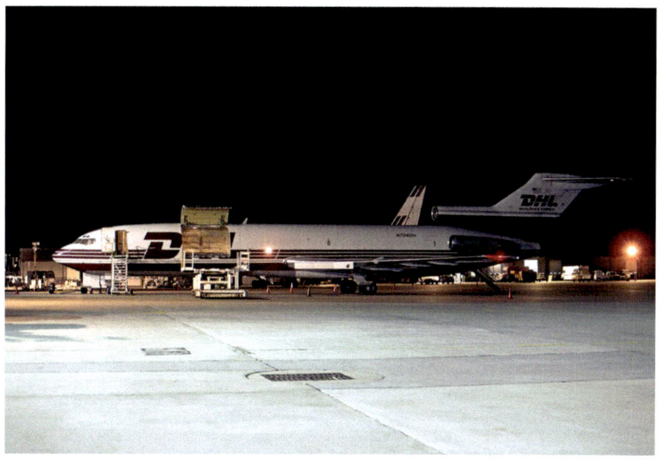

On the other side of the cargo ramp, DHL's 727-200 N724DH, which began its career with Air France, is ready for loading.

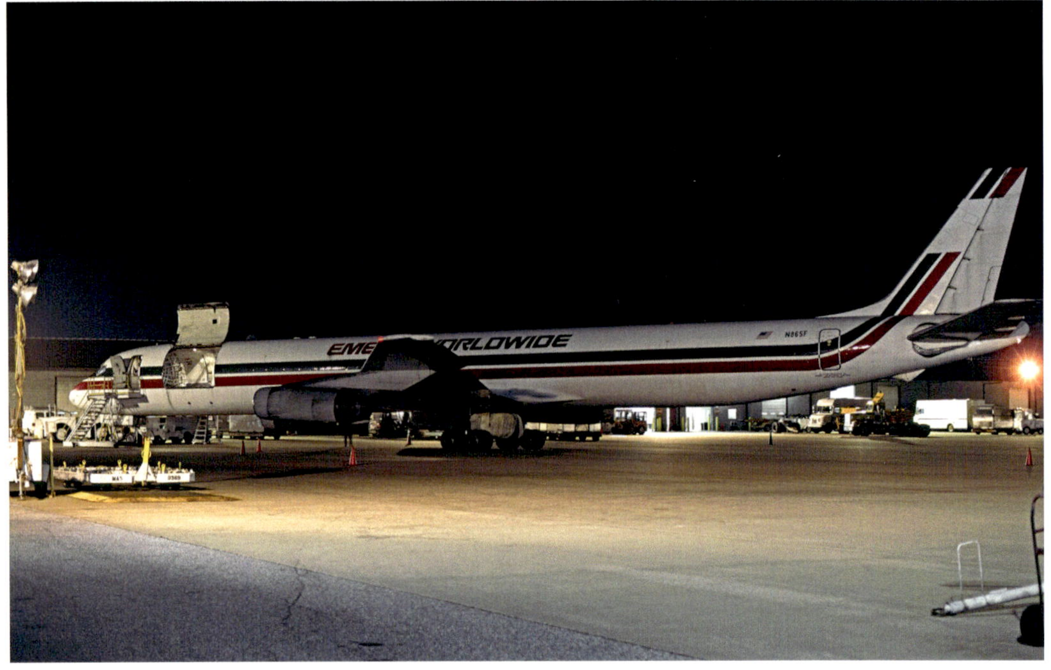

Behind the DHL 727, Emery Worldwide's DC-8-63F N865F is in the same status.

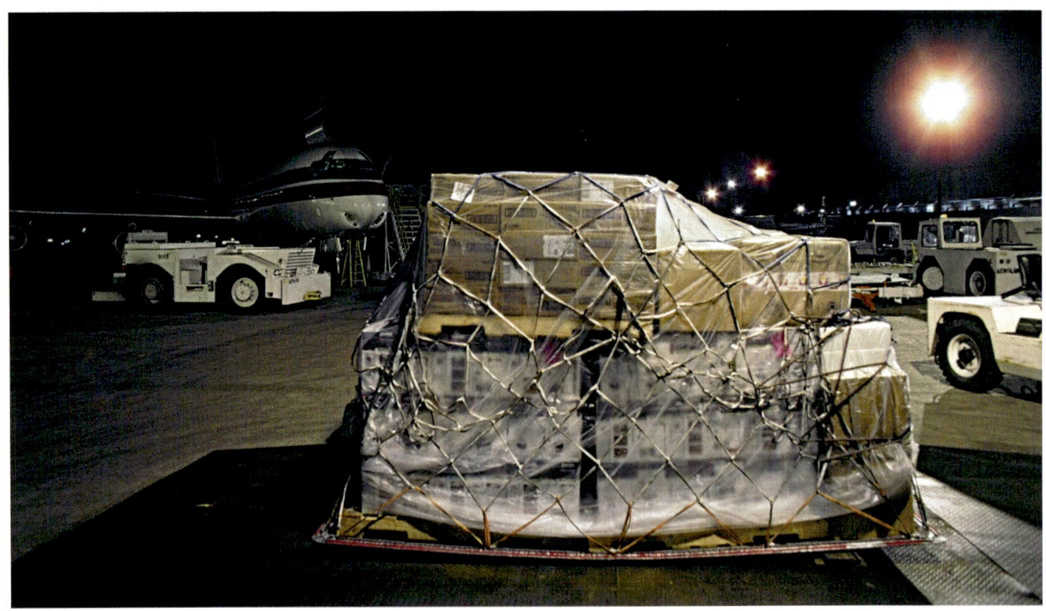

Here is a look at what is likely to be a load destined for the Emery DC-8. While "integrated" carriers such as FedEx and UPS handle the vast majority of their traffic on freighter aircraft in containers, the classic combination of "pallet and net" (in this case supplemented by plastic wrap) is still in use elsewhere.

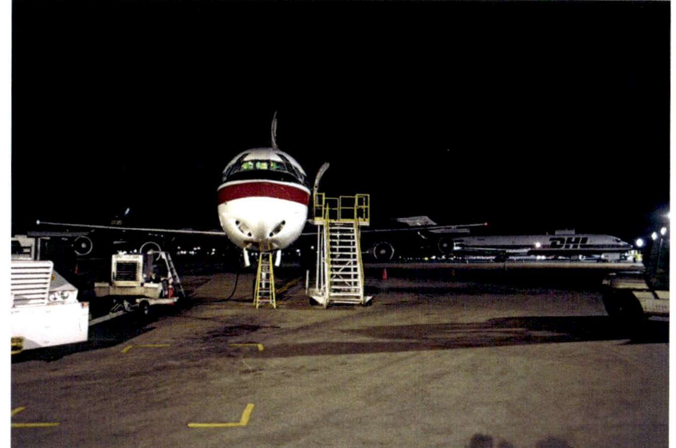

Here is another look at N865F and N724DH from a different perspective.

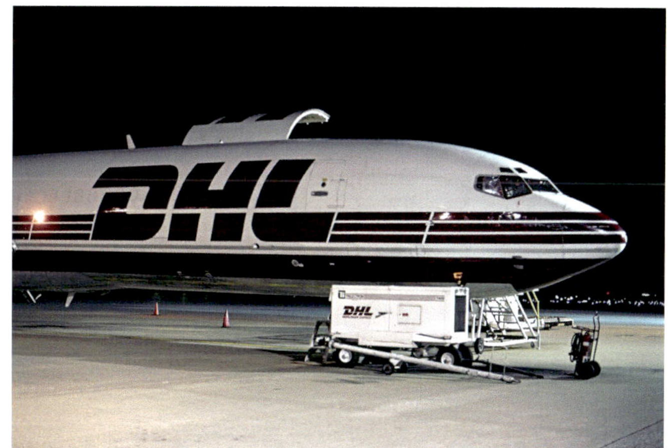

That is a very clean ramp where the DHL 727 is parked; the same description could be applied to the aircraft's livery as well.

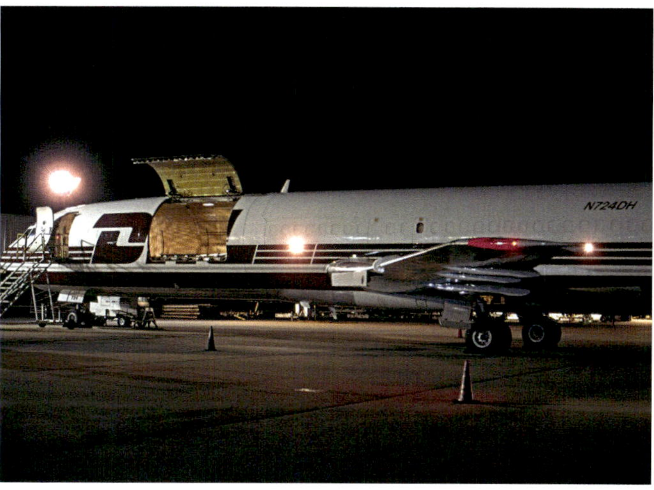

What's missing? The loader has been removed from the vicinity of N724DH, but likely will be back soon, along with the cargo for the evening's departure.

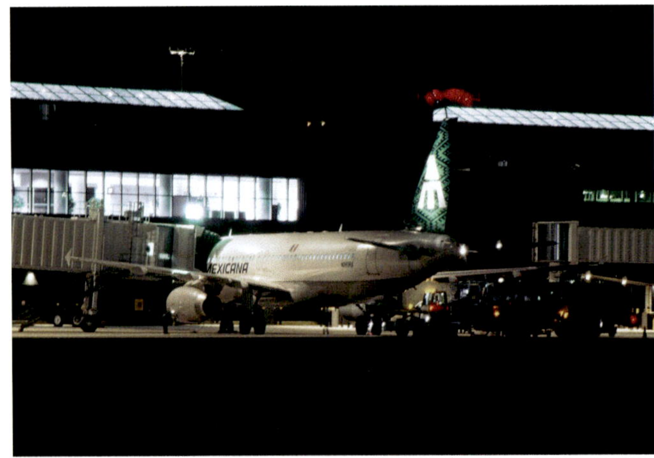

Over at Concourse E, Mexicana A320 N280RX has arrived, likely from a Mexican resort location.

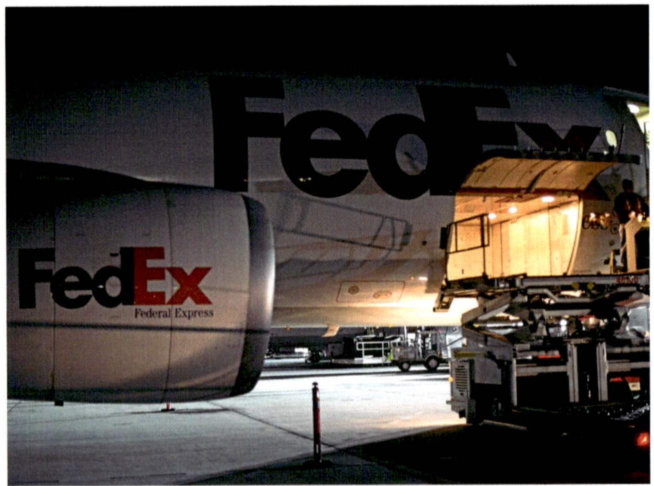

FedEx A300 N667FE is having cargo loaded into its forward belly pit.

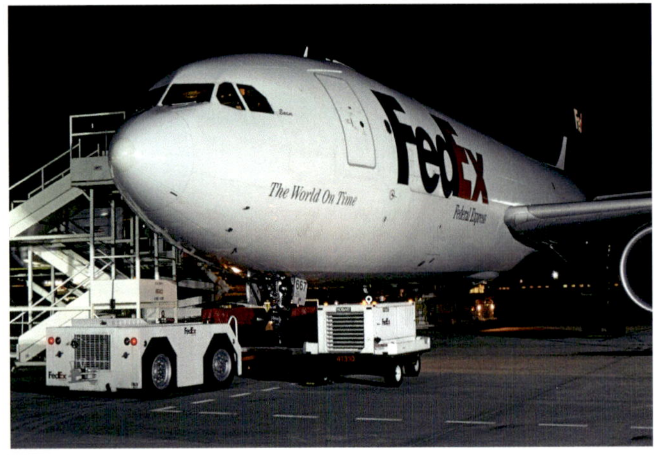

On the other side of the aircraft, however, the main deck cargo door is still shut.

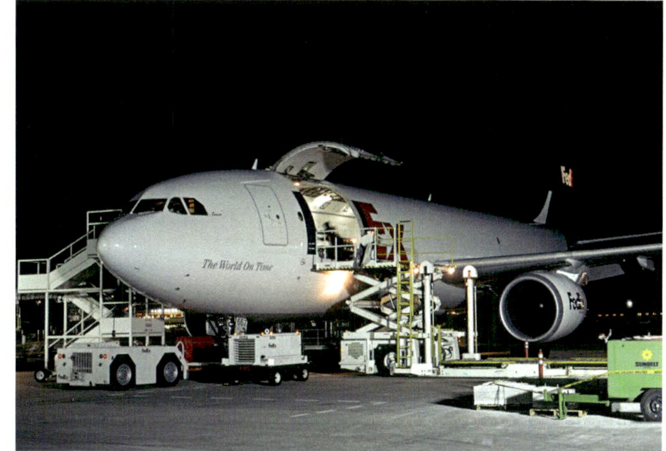

A short time later, however, it has been opened, and the loader positioned on the aircraft.

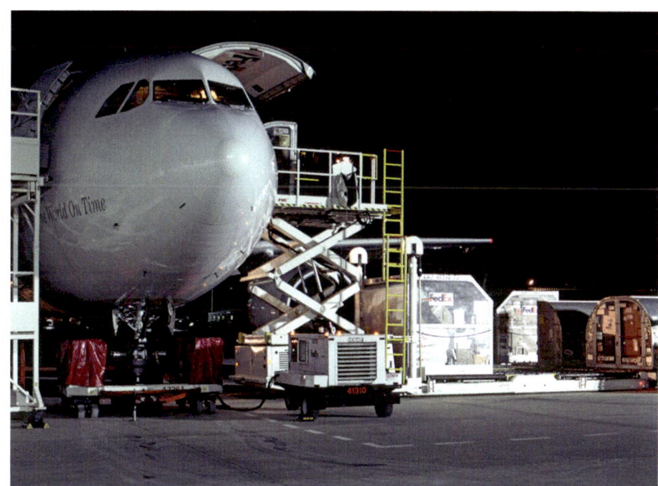

Containers being loaded into N667FE this evening are moved into position on the loader.

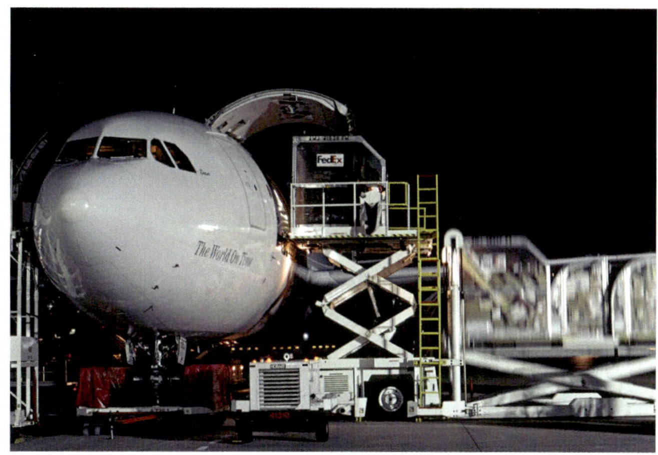

Next, the containers are lifted up to match the height of the cargo floor in the aircraft.

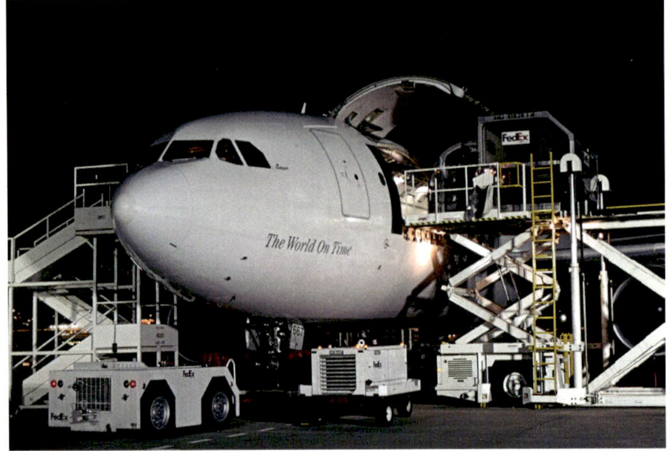

Finally, they are loaded into the aircraft through the main cargo door, and then pushed aft so that the process can be repeated until the aircraft is fully loaded.

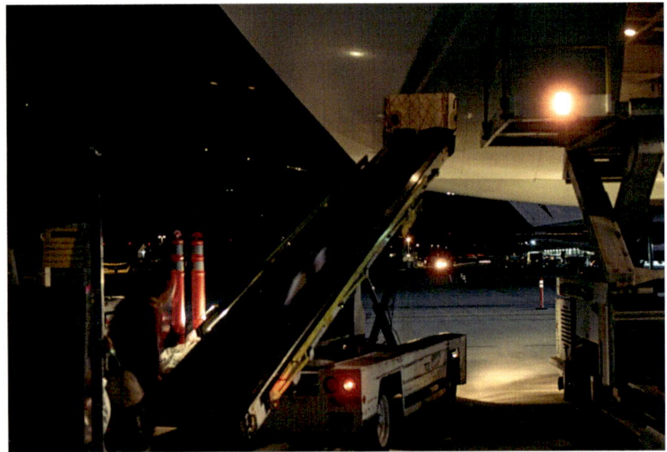

Back on the other side of the aircraft, a few small shipments are being loaded into the aft "bulk" cargo compartment (which is not capable of accepting even the smaller containers used for the main bellies), utilizing a belt loader like we have seen in conjunction with passenger aircraft servicing.

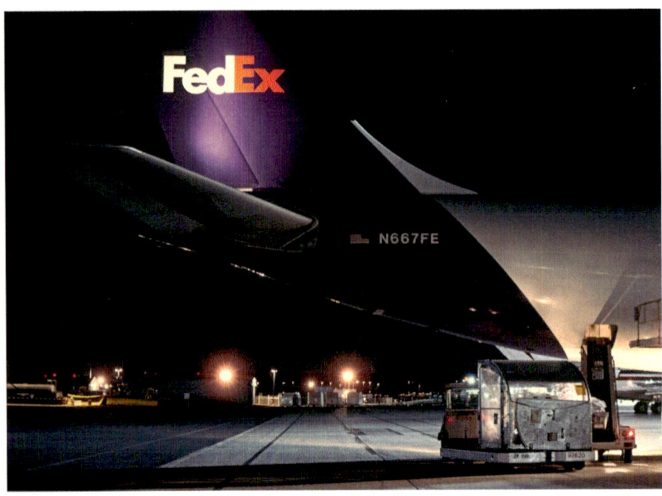

N667FE will soon be ready to undertake the flying portion of tonight's cargo movements; our evening is complete, however. I hope that you have enjoyed your look at the airside activities at BWI!